STITCHED
SAFARI

18 ADORABLE ANIMALS
TO MAKE WITH FELT

D0702275

Tomomi Maeda

D&C
David and Charles

www.stitchcraftcreate.co.uk

CALGARY PUBLIC LIBRARY

NOV   2013

Contents

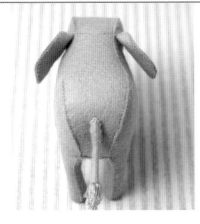

Elephants

Instructions page 45

An elephant never forgets, so remember to add these thoughtful details: floppy ears, a tufted tail, and a tremendous trunk that can be molded into playful shapes through the use of flexible wire.

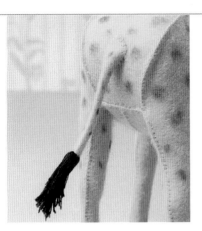

Giraffes

Instructions page 51

Spot the unique features on these giraffes from a mile away: fuzzy horns, fringed manes, and speckled coats hand-drawn as a finishing touch.

Gorilla

Instructions page 56

You're welcome to feed this gorilla anytime...how could you resist those endearingly long arms, tiny ears, and that adorable, life-like face?

Zebra

Instructions page 61

When you hear hoofbeats, think of this zebra. Use beige felt to accent his ears and hooves, then black embroidery floss to supply his signature stripes.

Kangaroos

Instructions page 65

Hop to it and make this mob of kangaroos, just don't skip over the fun details like the playfully long ears and tail or the little joey peeking out of mom's pouch.

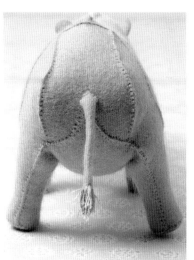

Rhinoceros

Instructions page 69

Watch out! This rhino is so cute he might cause a stampede. Check out those impressive horns, laughably large nostrils, and patchwork hide before this rhino rolls in the mud.

Panda

Instructions page 74

Keep an eye on your bamboo plants when this playful panda is around. The panda's black and white color scheme allows the special details to stand out, like those characteristic eye patches and contrasting gray paws.

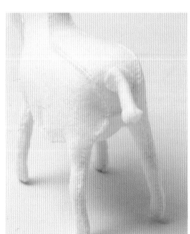

Goat

Instructions page 79

We've got your goat right here...and isn't he cute? No matter the color scheme, his whimsical features, such as the wispy beard made of embroidery floss or those long horns, really shine through.

Sheep

Instructions page 82

You'll love counting these sheep. With their fuzzy, woolen coats made of yarn and sweet facial features, these sheep are perfect for cuddling.

Cows

Instructions page 85

Have a cow over these bovine beauties! These cows are bursting with "udderly" adorable details, like free-form spots, pink muzzles, and swishing tails.

Pig

Instructions page 92

Pretty in pink, these felt beauties don't need any lipstick. With their little snouts and rotund bodies, these pigs are charming from nose to curly tail.

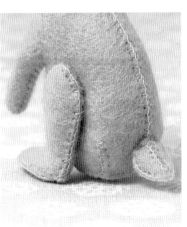

Rabbit

Instructions page 95

Who wouldn't want to pull one of these sweet rabbits out of a hat? With their big ears and little bodies, these happy hoppers stitch up in no time.

Dogs

Instructions page 98

Make every day a dog day with these two lovable members of the canine community. Create the Pug's adorably wrinkled face by pinching the felt and sewing very fine stitches. Give your Shiba her final touch of poise with her upright curled tail.

Cats

Instructions page 105

These felt felines are the cat's meow! Add curious details, like almond-shaped eyes, curled tails, and playful poses to complete these fun felt friends.

Penguin

Instructions page 111

There's no need to get dressed up for these penguins. Honor these wondrous waddlers by sewing them in crisp black, white, and gray felt, then add some final touches of red and orange. Wide-set webbed feet provide the perfect penguin stance.

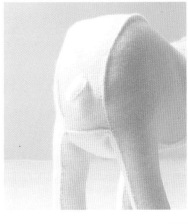

Polar Bears

Instructions page 115

With such sweet expressions, these polar bears would stand out anywhere, even in a snowstorm. Tiny little tails and delicately stitched faces complement their big white patchwork bodies—after admiring them, you may feel the urge to give a bear hug!

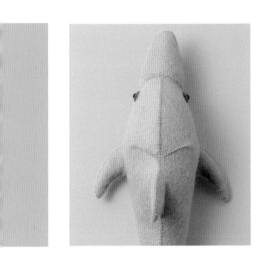  

Dolphin

Instructions page 122

Make a splash with this dolphin! Stitched flippers, fins, and a bottlenose serve as charming details on these friendly and fun-loving felt creatures.

Flamingo

Instructions page 125

These felt flamingoes will have you tickled pink! Handstitched with wonderfully wide wings and curvy bodies, all remarkably balanced on big yellow feet and long skinny legs, these flamingoes are both quirky and majestic.

Tools & Materials

Felt: Used for the body of all the animals. Sold at most craft stores, felt is available in wool, wool blends, and synthetic fibers.

Embroidery floss: Used to add details, such as manes, tails, and facial features.

Machine sewing thread: Used to sew the felt pieces together, machine sewing thread produces a neat finish.

Scissors: Used to cut the felt and thread. Small craft scissors are ideal since they allow more control when working with small pieces.

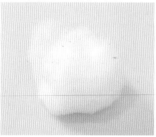

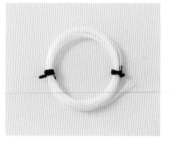

Tweezers: Used to stuff narrow areas.

Polyester stuffing: Used to stuff the animals.

Eye buttons: Used for the faces, these buttons are available in a wide variety of sizes.

Plastic wire: Used to provide shape and support. All of the animals in this book use 21-gauge plastic wire.

Cutting

1. Photocopy the templates.

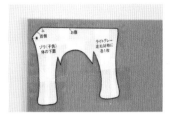

2. Cut out the photocopied templates and tape them to the felt.

3. Cut out the felt along the templates.

4. Lay out all the pieces to make sure you have everything you need for the project.

Sewing

Note: *All body parts will be sewn together with blanket stitch, unless otherwise noted. Refer to page 44 for more information on blanket stitch. You will see symbols such as ★ and ■. These are markers to help you align important points when sewing.*

1. Align the two body bottom pieces.

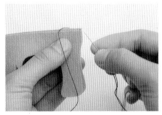

2. Insert a threaded needle between the two pieces, hiding the knot inside the felt.

Always insert the needle at a 90 degree angle to the felt.

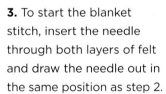

3. To start the blanket stitch, insert the needle through both layers of felt and draw the needle out in the same position as step 2.

Note: *In these photos, we have used contrasting color thread for visual clarity. When making the animals, refer to the materials list for the correct thread color.*

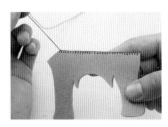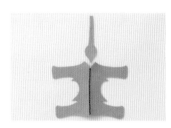

4. Insert the needle ⅛"
(0.3 cm) to the left of
the first stitch, make a
loop, and draw the needle
through the loop.

5. Continue sewing until
the seam is complete.

6. Align the head bottom
with the body bottom.

7. Start sewing the pieces
together along the right
edge.

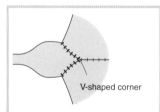

When sewing the
V-shaped corner, make
sure there is no gap
between the stitches at
the corner point, or you'll
end up with a hole.

8. Stop sewing just before
the V-shaped corner.

9. Align the pieces along
the left edge and continue
sewing from the V-shaped
corner.

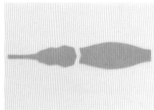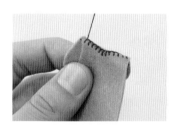

10. Continue sewing along
the left edge until the
seam is complete.

11. Align the head top with
the body top.

12. Repeat steps 7-10 to
sew the pieces together.

13. Align the head side
with the body side.

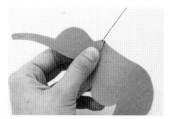

14. Start sewing the pieces together from the top. This will become the right side of the elephant.

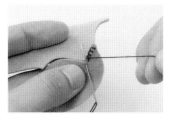

15. Make one stitch at the corner.

16. Repostition the felt to keep it aligned along the curve as you sew.

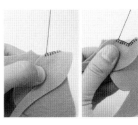

17. Continue repositioning the felt every few stitches to ensure that it is aligned along the curves.

18. Continue sewing until the seam is complete.

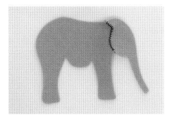

19. The right side is complete.

20. Repeat steps 13-19 to make the left side.

Make sure to align the pieces to create a mirror image when making the left side.

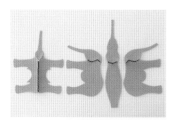

21. All four sides are complete.

22. Align the left side with the bottom.

23. Start sewing the pieces together from the trunk.

24. Reposition the felt to keep it aligned along the curve as you sew.

25. Continue sewing to the front foot.

Do not cut the thread. Using a new thread, start on the other side of this foot and continue sewing.

26. Align the pointed sections of the bottom with the indented sections of the side and sew.

27. Continue sewing to the back foot. Do not cut the thread.

28. Using the thread from step 25, sew a sole to the front leg.

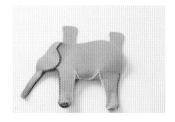

29. Sew the body side and body bottom together along back leg. Using the thread from step 27, sew a sole to the back leg.

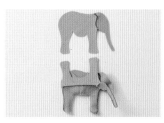

30. Align the right side with the elephant.

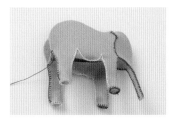

31. Repeat steps 23-29 to sew the pieces together and attach the soles.

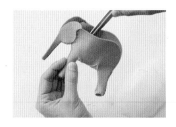

32. Firmly stuff the feet.

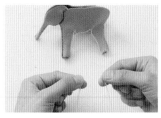

33. Bend two 5½" (14 cm) long wires into U-shapes.

34. Insert the wires into the legs and stuff.

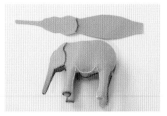

35. Align the top with the elephant.

36. Start sewing the pieces together from the trunk and continue to the back leg.

37. On the other side, sew the pieces together along half of the trunk only. Do not cut the thread.

38. Roll up a ¾" (2 cm) square piece of felt and insert it into the tip of the trunk.

39. Sew around the tip of the trunk to secure the roll of felt in place.

40. Stuff the trunk.

41. Bend the tip of a 2¾" (7 cm) wire into a U-shape and insert it into the trunk. Add more stuffing if necessary.

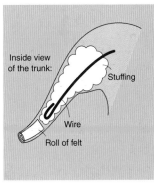

Inside view of the trunk:

Stuffing

Wire

Roll of felt

42. Sew the elephant closed from the trunk to the rear end, stuffing as you work.

Add stuffing every few stitches to define the shape of each body part. Firmly stuff the elephant so there is no empty space in the body.

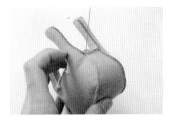

43. Sew the elephant closed along the rear end.

Finishing Touches

Ears

1. Using two colors of felt, cut out two symmetrical sets of ears.

2. For each ear, layer the two colors of felt and sew together around all four edges. At the top of the ear, fold the edge over about ¼" (0.5 cm) and make a few stitches to secure the fold.

3. Sew the ears to the head along the seam.

4. The ears are complete!

Eyes

1. For each eye, use a large needle to puncture a hole in the felt. Insert an eye button through the hole and glue it to the felt. Trim the felt into a circle.

2. Puncture holes in the head at the positions to attach the eyes.

3. Insert the eye buttons in the holes and glue to secure in place.

Your animal's facial expression will change depending upon the position of the eyes. Check to make sure the eyes are balanced before gluing them in place.

Tail

1. Cut out the tail.

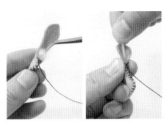

2. Fold the tail in half widthwise. Align the edges and sew, stuffing as you work. Insert a 1" (2.5 cm) wire.

3. Leave the end of the tail open. This side will attach to the body. Sew around the end in a circle. Do not cut the thread.

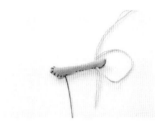

4. Using embroidery floss, make a 1¼" (3 cm) diameter loop at the tip of the tail.

5. Make several more loops of similar size.

6. Cut the end of the loops.

7. Spread the embroidery floss apart and apply a dab of glue to the tail.

8. Gather the embroidery floss around the dab of glue.

9. Trim the tail into shape.

Trim the embroidery floss at an angle to create a realistic looking tail.

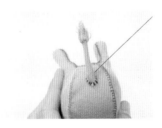

10. Glue the tail in place and sew to the body using the thread from step 3.

11. The elephant is complete!

Mane

Note: *This technique is used for the zebra and giraffe.*

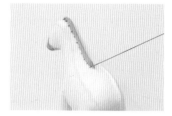

1. Hemstitch the mane piece to the body.

2. Using 6 strands of embroidery floss, make loops around the mane piece, stitching through the body.

3. Make sure there are no gaps between the loops.

4. Cut the ends of the loops.

5. Spread the embroidery floss apart and apply a line of glue on each side of the mane piece.

6. Gather the embroidery floss around the glue.

7. Trim the mane into shape.

8. Let the glue dry completely.

Ears

Note: *This technique is used for the pig, giraffe, zebra, kangaroo, rhino, goat, sheep, shiba, cat, and polar bear.*

  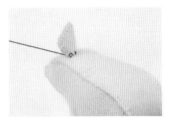 

1. Layer the two colors of felt and sew the edges together.

2. Fold the ear in half inwardly and make two stitches at the base, stitching through both layers, to secure the fold.

3. Sew the ear to the body.

4. By securing the fold in place before attaching the ear to body, the ear will stand upright.

Legs

Note: *This technique is used for the kangaroo, rabbit, cat, and flamingo.*

1. Sew the two pieces of felt together along half of the leg. Do not cut the thread. Bend the plastic wire into the shape of the leg and insert.

2. Fill the leg with stuffing. Finish sewing the leg together, leaving the bottom edge open.

3. Align the sole with the leg and sew.

4. The plastic wire gives the leg a more realistic, dimensional shape.

Stitch Guide

Blanket Stitch

This overcast stitch is made by inserting the needle near the edge of the fabric and pulling the needle through the loop created by the thread. Throughout this book, blanket stitch is used to sew the felt pieces together.

Note that the horizontal line created when blanket stitching has been omitted from the instruction diagrams throughout the book for the purpose of visual clarity.

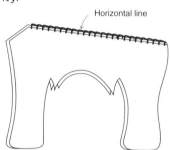

Starting a New Thread When Blanket Stitching

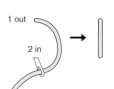

1. When your thread runs out, insert the needle through one layer of felt. On the wrong side, make a knot and cut the thread.

2. Using a new thread with a knot at the end, draw the needle out on the right side of the felt at the same position as step 1.

3. Make one blanket stitch, inserting the needle at the same position as step 1. Continue blanket stitching.

4. Note: When you change thread, the first and last stitches overlap.

Straight Stitch

This basic stitch is made by passing the needle in and out of the fabric. The straight stitch is used to add details to the animals, such as mouths and stripes.

Sew continuously

Satin Stitch

This embroidery technique is created by parallel rows of straight stitches positioned closed together. The satin stitch is used to add facial features, such as noses.

Elephants

Shown on page 4

Materials

Adult Elephant

- Felt pieces
  - Pale gray: Four 8" x 8" (20 x 20 cm)
  - Pink: 2¾" x 4" (7 x 10 cm)
  - Beige: ¾" x 1½" (2 x 4 cm)
  - Off-white: 1½" x 2" (4 x 5 cm)
- Machine sewing thread in gray and off-white
- 6-strand embroidery floss in light gray
- 37½" (95 cm) of 21-gauge plastic wire
- Two ¼" (0.5 cm) diameter black eye buttons
- Polyester stuffing
- Quick-dry tacky glue

Baby Elephant

- Felt pieces
  - Light gray: Two 8" x 8" (20 x 20 cm)
  - Pink: 1½" x 2½" (4 x 6 cm)
  - Beige: ¾" x 1½" (2 x 4 cm)
- Machine sewing thread in gray
- 6-strand embroidery floss in light gray
- 15" (38 cm) of 21-gauge plastic wire
- Two ¼" (0.4 cm) diameter black eye buttons
- Polyester stuffing
- Quick-dry tacky glue

Cutting Instructions

Trace and cut out the following templates on pattern sheet A:

Adult Elephant

Pale Gray Felt
- Body bottom (cut 2)
- Head bottom (cut 1)
- Body top (cut 1)
- Head top (cut 1)
- Head side (cut 2)
- Body side (cut 2)
- Soles (cut 4)
- Ears (cut 2)
- Tail (cut 1)

Beige Felt
- Eye pieces (cut 2)

Off-White Felt
- Tusks (cut 4)
- Tusk base (cut 2)

Pink Felt
- Ears (cut 2)

Baby Elephant

Light Gray Felt
- Body bottom (cut 2)
- Head bottom (cut 1)
- Body top (cut 1)
- Head top (cut 1)
- Head side (cut 2)
- Body side (cut 2)
- Soles (cut 4)
- Ears (cut 2)
- Tail (cut 1)

Beige Felt
- Eye pieces (cut 2)

Pink Felt
- Ears (cut 2)

Finished Project

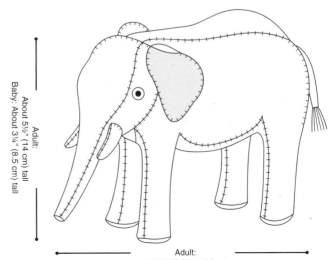

Adult: About 5½" (14 cm) tall
Baby: About 3¼" (8.5 cm) tall

Adult:
About 7" (18 cm) long
Baby: About 4¼" (11 cm) long

* Tusks are for adult elephant only.

Sew the head and body pieces together.

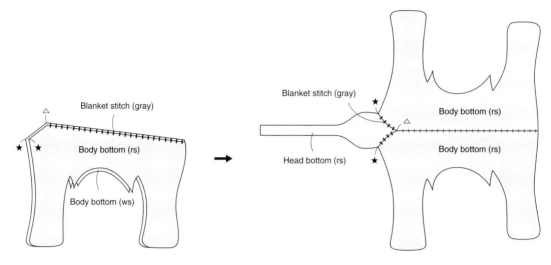

1. Sew two **body bottom** pieces together (△).

2. Align **head bottom** with **body bottom** (★) and sew to form elephant bottom.

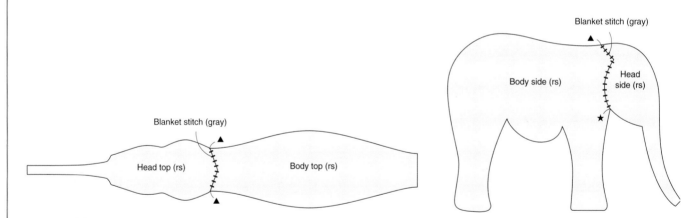

3. Align **head top** with **body top** (▲) and sew to form elephant top.

4. Align **head side** with **body side** (▲ and ★) and sew to form one elephant side. Repeat for other side.

Attach the sides and bottom.

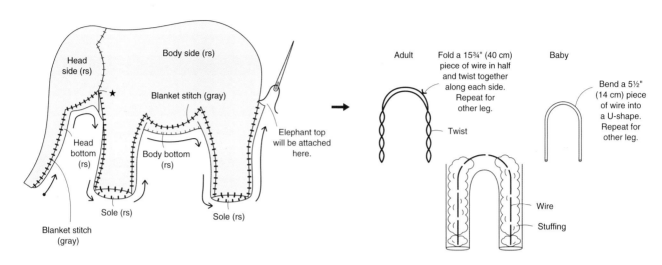

1. Align one elephant side with elephant bottom. Sew body and **soles**, as shown on pages 37-38. Repeat for other elephant side.

2. Firmly stuff feet. Bend wires into shape, as shown in diagram. Insert wires and more stuffing into legs.

Attach the top and finish the trunk.

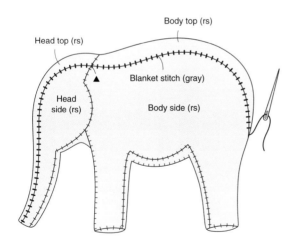

1. Align elephant top with one elephant side and sew from trunk to rear end. On other side, sew pieces together along half of trunk only. Do not cut thread.

Attach the top and finish the trunk (continued).

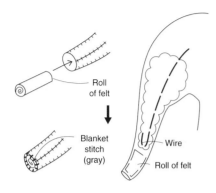

Roll
of felt

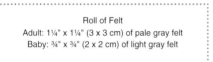

Blanket
stitch
(gray)

Wire

Roll of felt

Wire
Adult: About 4" (10 cm)
Baby: About 2¾" (7 cm)

2. Roll up a square piece of felt, insert into trunk, and sew around trunk tip to secure. Stuff trunk. Bend tip of wire into a U-shape and insert into trunk. Add more stuffing if necessary.

Roll of Felt
Adult: 1¼" x 1¼" (3 x 3 cm) of pale gray felt
Baby: ¾" x ¾" (2 x 2 cm) of light gray felt

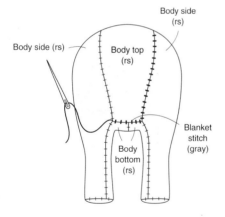

Body side (rs)

Body side
(rs)

Body top
(rs)

Blanket
stitch
(gray)

Body
bottom
(rs)

3. Sew elephant closed from trunk to rear end, stuffing as you work.

Finish the face.

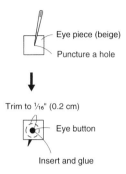

Eye piece (beige)
Puncture a hole

Trim to 1/16" (0.2 cm)

Eye button

Insert and glue

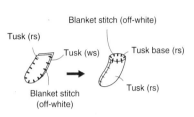

Blanket stitch (off-white)

Tusk (rs)

Tusk (ws)

Tusk base (rs)

Tusk (rs)

Blanket stitch
(off-white)

1. Use a large needle to puncture a hole in each **eye piece**. Insert eye buttons through holes and glue to felt. Trim each piece of felt into a circle that is about 1/16" (0.2 cm) wider than eye button.

2. For each tusk, sew two **tusk** pieces together and stuff. For each tusk, sew **tusk base** and **tusk** together. Note: tusks are for adult elephant only.

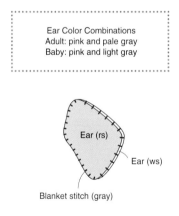

Ear Color Combinations
Adult: pink and pale gray
Baby: pink and light gray

Ear (rs)

Ear (ws)

Blanket stitch (gray)

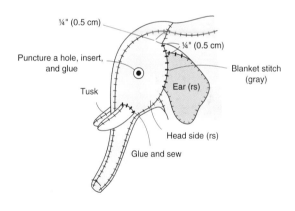

1/4" (0.5 cm)

1/4" (0.5 cm)

Puncture a hole, insert, and glue

Blanket stitch (gray)

Ear (rs)

Tusk

Head side (rs)

Glue and sew

3. For each **ear**, layer two colors of felt and sew together around all edges.

4. At top of each **ear**, fold edge over about 1/4" (0.5 cm) and make a few stitches to secure fold. Sew ears to head. Glue **tusks** in place and sew to head. Puncture holes in head at position to attach eyes. Insert eye buttons and glue to secure.

Make and attach the tail.

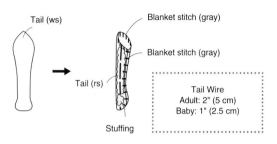

Tail (ws)

Tail (rs)

Blanket stitch (gray)

Blanket stitch (gray)

Tail Wire
Adult: 2" (5 cm)
Baby: 1" (2.5 cm)

Stuffing

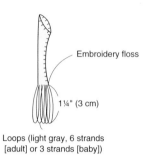

Embroidery floss

1¼" (3 cm)

Loops (light gray, 6 strands
[adult] or 3 strands [baby])

1. Fold **tail** in half widthwise and sew edges together, stuffing as you work. Insert wire. Leave end of tail open. Sew around end in a circle. Do not cut thread.

2. Make 1¼" (3 cm) loops at tail tip. Cut ends of loops.

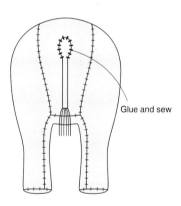

Glue and sew

3. Spread embroidery floss apart and apply a dab of glue to tail. Gather embroidery floss around dab of glue and trim tail into shape. Glue tail in place and sew to body.

Materials

Adult Giraffe
- Felt pieces
  - Yellow: Three 8" x 8" (20 x 20 cm)
  - Beige: 1¼" x 2" (3 x 5 cm)
  - Reddish brown: ¾" x 4" (2 x 10 cm)
  - Light brown: 2" x 4" (5 x 10 cm)
- Machine sewing thread in yellow and light brown
- 6-strand embroidery floss in reddish brown, beige, and brown
- 21¼" (54 cm) of 21-gauge plastic wire
- Two ¼" (0.4 cm) diameter black eye buttons
- Polyester stuffing
- Quick-dry tacky glue
- Brown eyebrow pencil

Baby Giraffe
- Felt pieces
  - Light yellow: 8" x 8" (20 x 20 cm)
  - Beige: 1¼" x 2" (3 x 5 cm)
  - Reddish brown: ⅜" x 2¾" (1 x 7 cm)
- Machine sewing thread in yellow
- 6-strand embroidery floss in reddish brown, beige, and brown
- 15½" (39 cm) of 21-gauge plastic wire
- Two ⅛" (0.3 cm) diameter black eye buttons
- Polyester stuffing
- Quick-dry tacky glue
- Brown eyebrow pencil

Giraffes
Shown on page 6

Cutting Instructions
Trace and cut out the following templates on pattern sheet A:

Adult Giraffe
Yellow Felt
- Head bottom (cut 1)
- Head side (cut 2)
- Head top (cut 1)
- Body bottom (cut 2)
- Body side (cut 2)
- Body top (cut 1)
- Ears (cut 2)
- Horns (cut 4)
- Tail (cut 1)

Beige Felt
- Ears (cut 2)
- Eye pieces (cut 2)

Reddish Brown Felt
- Mane piece (cut 1)

Light Brown Felt
- Hoof sides (cut 4)
- Hoof bottoms (cut 4)

Baby Giraffe
Light Yellow Felt
- Head bottom (cut 1)
- Head side (cut 2)
- Head top (cut 1)
- Body bottom (cut 2)
- Body side (cut 2)
- Body top (cut 1)
- Ears (cut 2)
- Horns (cut 4)
- Tail (cut 1)

Beige Felt
- Ears (cut 2)
- Eye pieces (cut 2)

Reddish Brown Felt
- Mane piece (cut 1)

Finished Project

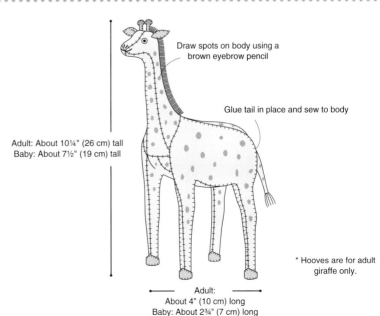

Draw spots on body using a brown eyebrow pencil

Glue tail in place and sew to body

Adult: About 10¼" (26 cm) tall
Baby: About 7½" (19 cm) tall

Adult:
About 4" (10 cm) long
Baby: About 2¾" (7 cm) long

* Hooves are for adult giraffe only.

Make the head.

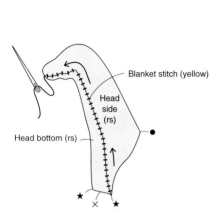
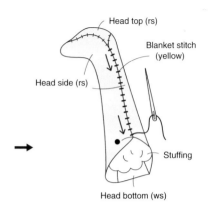
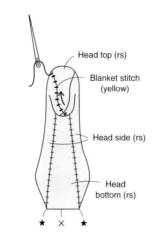

1. Align one **head side** with **head bottom** and sew. Repeat for other **head side**.

2. Align **head top** with one **head side** and sew together.

3. Align **head top** with remaining **head side** and sew together from nose to neck base, stitching two **head sides** together down length of neck (●) and stuffing as you work.

Make the body.

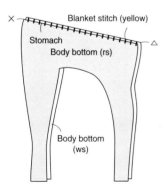
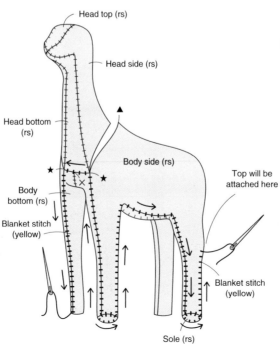

1. Sew two **body bottom** pieces together.

2. Align one **body side** with **body bottom**, then align **head bottom** with **body bottom** (★) and sew together along front legs, following direction indicated by arrows in diagram. Sew together along back legs, following direction indicated by arrows in diagram. Repeat for other **body side**. For adult giraffe, align each **sole** with each leg and sew. For baby giraffe, stitch legs closed.

Make the body (continued).

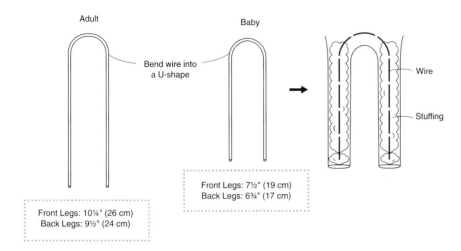

Adult

Baby

Bend wire into a U-shape

Wire

Stuffing

Front Legs: 7½" (19 cm)
Back Legs: 6¾" (17 cm)

Front Legs: 10¼" (26 cm)
Back Legs: 9½" (24 cm)

3. Stuff feet. Bend wires into two U-shaped pieces, as shown in diagram. Insert wires into front and back legs. Add more stuffing.

Finish the body.

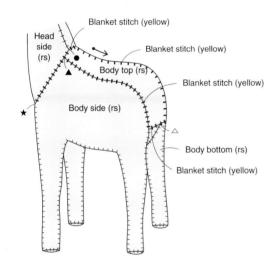

Head side (rs)

Blanket stitch (yellow)

Blanket stitch (yellow)

Body top (rs)

Blanket stitch (yellow)

Body side (rs)

Body bottom (rs)

Blanket stitch (yellow)

1. Align one **body side** with **body top** (▲) and sew. Align remaining **body side** with **body top** and sew together along base of neck only, using 4-5 stitches. Do not cut thread. Align head with body and sew. Sew from neck base to rear end, stuffing as you work. Stuff bottom. Sew giraffe closed along rear end.

Finish the face.

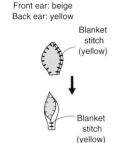

Front ear: beige
Back ear: yellow

Blanket stitch (yellow)

Blanket stitch (yellow)

1. For each **ear**, layer two colors of felt and sew together. Fold each ear in half inwardly and make two stitches at base, stitching through both edges, to secure the fold.

Eye piece (beige)

Puncture a hole

Trim to ¹⁄₁₆" (0.2 cm)

Eye button

Insert and glue

2. Use a large needle to puncture a hole in each felt **eye piece**. Insert eye buttons through holes and glue to felt. Trim each piece of felt into a circle that is about ¹⁄₁₆" (0.2 cm) wider than eye button.

Finish the face (continued).

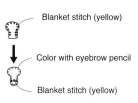

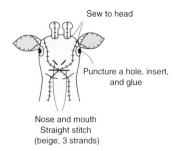

3. For each horn, sew two **horn** pieces together, leaving one edge open. Color top of horns using brown eyebrow pencil. Stuff, then sew around base of each horn.

4. Sew **ears** and **horns** to head. Embroider nose and mouth. Hide knot in mane. Puncture holes in head at position to attach eyes. Insert eye buttons and glue to secure.

Make the mane.

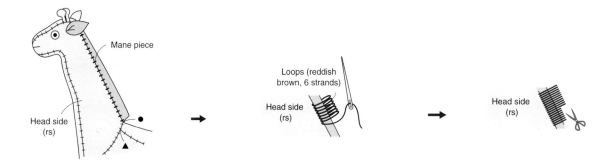

1. Hemstitch **mane piece** to neck.

2. Make loops around **mane piece**, stitching through **head side.**

3. Cut ends of loops. Spread embroidery floss apart and apply a line of glue to each side of mane piece. Gather embroidery floss around glue. Trim mane into shape.

Make the tail.

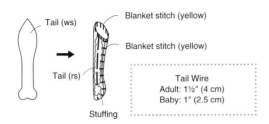 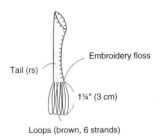

1. Fold **tail** in half widthwise and sew edges together, stuffing as you work. Insert wire. Leave end of tail open. Sew around end in a circle. Do not cut thread.

2. Make 1¼" (3 cm) loops at tail tip. Cut ends of loops. Spread embroidery floss apart and apply a dab of glue to tail. Gather embroidery floss around dab of glue and trim tail into shape. Glue tail in place and sew to body, as shown in finished project diagram on page 51.

Make the hooves (for the adult giraffe only).

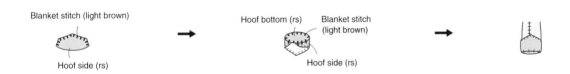

1. Blanket stitch along top of each **hoof side**.

2. Align each **hoof side** with a **hoof bottom** and sew.

3. Glue hooves to **soles**.

Finish the giraffe.

Draw spots on body using a brown eyebrow pencil, as shown in finished project diagram on page 51.

Gorilla Shown on page 8

Materials

- Felt pieces
  - Dark brown: Two 8" x 8" (20 x 20 cm)
  - Black: 4" x 4" (10 x 10 cm)
  - Green: ⅜" x ¾" (1 x 2 cm)
- Machine sewing thread in dark brown and black
- 6-strand embroidery floss in dark gray
- Two ⅛" (0.3 cm) diameter black eye buttons
- Polyester stuffing
- Quick-dry tacky glue

Cutting Instructions

Trace and cut out the following templates on pattern sheet A:

Dark Brown Felt
- Outer face (cut 1)
- Head (cut 2)
- Body front (cut 2)
- Body back (cut 1)
- Body side (cut 2)
- Ears (cut 2)
- Nose (cut 2)
- Outer arm (cut 2)
- Inner arm (cut 2)
- Outer leg (cut 2)
- Inner leg (cut 2)

- Arm bottom (cut 2)
- Leg bottom (cut 2)

Black Felt
- Inner face (cut 1)
- Ears (cut 2)
- Mouth (cut 1)
- Mouth lining (cut 1)
- Chest (cut 1)
- Hands/feet (cut 4)

Green Felt
- Eye pieces (cut 2)

Finished Project

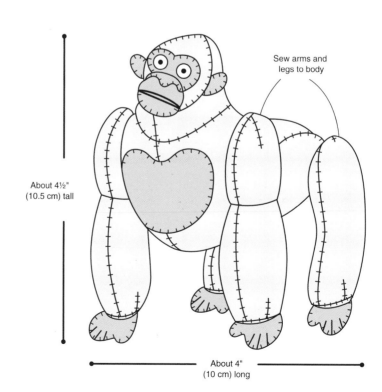

About 4½" (10.5 cm) tall

Sew arms and legs to body

About 4" (10 cm) long

Make the head.

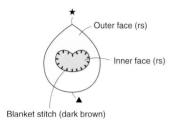

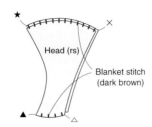

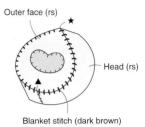

1. Layer **inner face** on top of **outer face** and sew.

2. Sew two **head** pieces together along top and bottom.

3. Align **head** with **outer face** and sew.

Make the body.

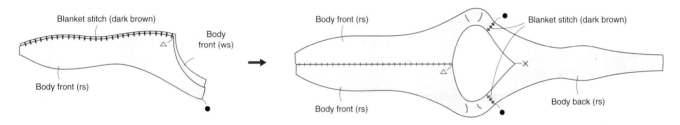

1. Sew two **body front** pieces together.

2. Align **body front** with **body back** (●) and sew.

Attach the head and the body.

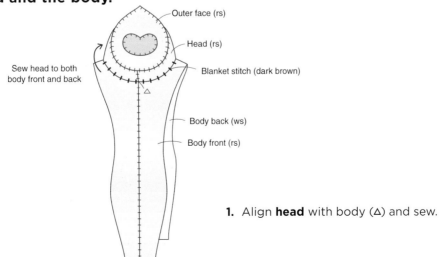

1. Align **head** with body (△) and sew.

Attach the head and the body (continued).

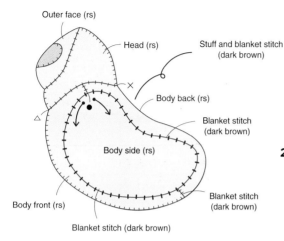

2. Align one **body side** with **body front** and sew, then align with **body back** and sew (●). Repeat for other **body side**, stuffing as you work. Align **body front** and **body back** and sew gorilla together along bottom.

Finish the face.

1. For each **ear**, layer two colors of felt and sew together around all edges

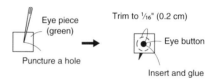

2. Use a large needle to puncture a hole in each felt **eye piece**. Insert eye buttons through holes and glue to felt eye pieces. Trim each piece of felt into a circle that is about 1/16" (0.2 cm) wider than eye button.

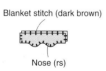

3. Align two **nose** pieces and sew together around all edges.

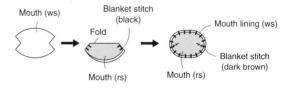

4. Fold **mouth** piece in half. Sew along two short sides of mouth piece to form darts. Align **mouth** with **mouth lining** and sew, stuffing as you work.

Finish the face (continued).

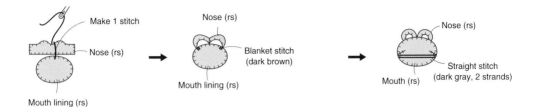

5. Align **nose** on top of **mouth** and make one stitch around center of nose, securing two pieces. Using your index finger, raise ends of nose piece and sew to mouth to form nostrils. Flip piece over and embroider mouth.

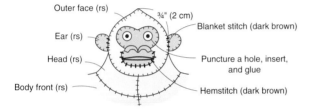

6. Layer **nose** and **mouth** on top of **outer face** and sew. Sew both **ears** to **outer face** along existing seams, about ¾" (2 cm) from top of head. Puncture holes in head at position to attach eyes. Insert eye buttons and glue to secure in place.

Make the chest.

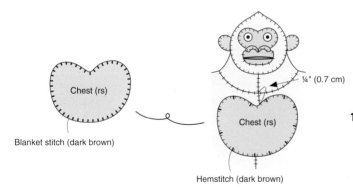

1. Blanket stitch around edge of **chest**. Layer **chest** on top of **body front**, about ¼" (0.7 cm) from neck and sew.

Make the arms, legs, hands, and feet.

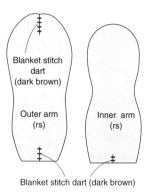

Blanket stitch dart (dark brown)

Outer arm (rs)

Inner arm (rs)

Blanket stitch dart (dark brown)

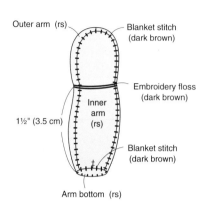

Outer arm (rs)

Blanket stitch (dark brown)

Embroidery floss (dark brown)

Inner arm (rs)

1½" (3.5 cm)

Blanket stitch (dark brown)

Arm bottom (rs)

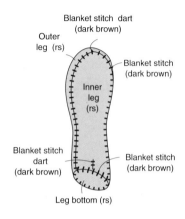

Blanket stitch dart (dark brown)

Outer leg (rs)

Blanket stitch (dark brown)

Inner leg (rs)

Blanket stitch dart (dark brown)

Blanket stitch (dark brown)

Leg bottom (rs)

1. Align darts on both **outer and inner arms** and sew.

2. Align **outer arm** with **inner arm**, sew, and stuff. Align **arm bottom** and sew. Wrap embroidery floss around arm twice about 1½" (3.5 cm) from arm bottom, securing by stitching into arm. Repeat for other arm.

3. Align darts on both **outer and inner legs** and sew. Align **outer leg** with **inner leg**, sew, and stuff. Align **leg bottom** and sew. Repeat for other leg.

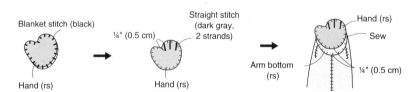

Blanket stitch (black)

Hand (rs)

¼" (0.5 cm)

Straight stitch (dark gray, 2 strands)

Hand (rs)

Hand (rs)

Sew

Arm bottom (rs)

¼" (0.5 cm)

4. Sew two **hand** pieces together around all edges. Embroider both sides of hand. Align **hand** so it extends past arm and sew to **arm bottom**. Repeat to make other hand and two **feet**. Sew arms and the legs to body, as shown in finished project diagram on page 56.

Materials

- Felt pieces
  - Off-white: Two 8" x 8" (20 x 20 cm)
  - Black: 2½" x 2½" (6 x 6 cm)
  - Beige: 2½" x 3¼" (6 x 8 cm)
  - Brown: ⅜" x ¾" (1 x 2 cm)
- Machine sewing thread in off-white, black, and light brown
- 6-strand embroidery floss in black and dark gray
- 14½" (37 cm) of 21-gauge plastic wire
- Two ¼" (0.4 cm) diameter black eye buttons
- Polyester stuffing
- Quick-dry tacky glue

Zebra Shown on page 10

Cutting Instructions

Trace and cut out the following templates on pattern sheet A:

Off-White Felt
- Body bottom (cut 1)
- Body side (cut 2)
- Body top (cut 1)
- Soles (cut 4)
- Ears (cut 2)
- Tail (cut 1)

Black Felt
- Nose (cut 1)
- Mane piece (cut 1)

Beige Felt
- Ears (cut 2)
- Hoof side (cut 4)
- Hoof bottom (cut 4)

Brown Felt
- Eye pieces (cut 2)

Finished Project

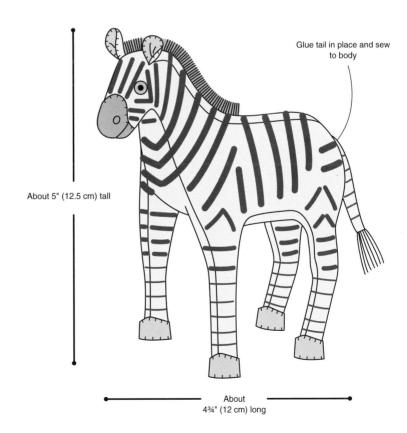

Glue tail in place and sew to body

About 5" (12.5 cm) tall

About 4¾" (12 cm) long

Make the body.

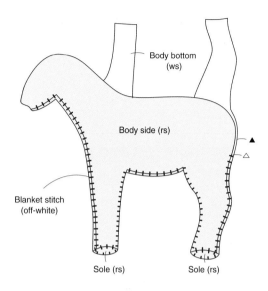

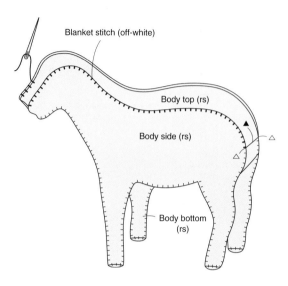

1. Align one **body side** with **body bottom**. Sew body and **soles**, as shown on page 37-38. Repeat for other **body side**.

2. Align one **body side** with **body top** and sew from nose to rear end. Align remaining **body side** with **body top** and sew together along nose only, using 4-5 stitches. Do not cut thread.

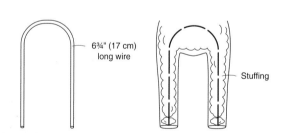

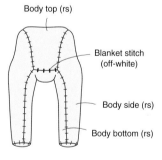

3. Stuff feet. Bend wires into two 6¾" (17 cm) U-shaped pieces. Insert wires into legs. Add more stuffing.

4. Stuff bottom. Sew zebra closed from nose to rear end.

Make the nose.

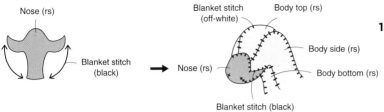

1. Align nose darts as indicated by arrows in diagram and sew. Sew nose to zebra.

Embroider the stripes.

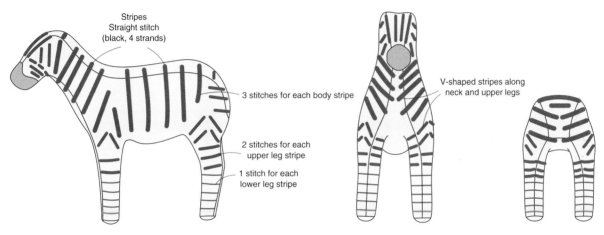

1. Starting at center of body top, embroider stripes along **body top** and **body side**. Make three stitches for each stripe along body, two stitches for each stripe along upper legs, and one stitch for each stripe along lower legs. Stitch stripes in a V-shape along neck and upper legs. Hide knots in mane, tail, or soles. Repeat for other side.

Make the mane.

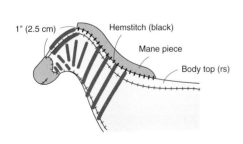

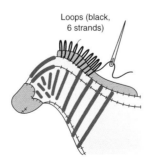

1. Hemstitch **mane piece** to neck.

2. Make loops around **mane piece**, stitching through **body top**. Cut ends of loops. Spread embroidery floss apart and apply a line of glue to each side of mane piece. Gather embroidery floss around glue. Trim mane into shape.

Finish the face.

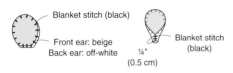

Blanket stitch (black)

Front ear: beige
Back ear: off-white

¼" (0.5 cm)

Blanket stitch (black)

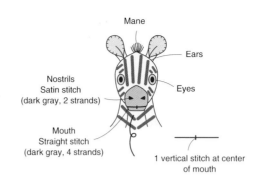

Mane

Ears

Nostrils
Satin stitch
(dark gray, 2 strands)

Eyes

Mouth
Straight stitch
(dark gray, 4 strands)

1 vertical stitch at center of mouth

1. For each **ear**, layer two colors of felt and sew together around all edges. Fold each ear in half inwardly and make two stitches at base, stitching through both edges, to secure fold.

2. Sew **ears** to top of head. Embroider nostrils and mouth. Make one small vertical stitch at center of mouth. Hide knots in mane. Refer to page 40 to make and attach eyes.

Make the tail.

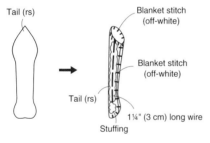

Tail (rs)

Blanket stitch
(off-white)

Blanket stitch
(off-white)

Tail (rs)

1¼" (3 cm) long wire

Stuffing

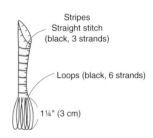

Stripes
Straight stitch
(black, 3 strands)

Loops (black, 6 strands)

1¼" (3 cm)

1. Fold **tail** in half widthwise and sew edges together, stuffing as you work. Insert wire. Add more stuffing. Leave end of tail open. This end will attach to body. Sew around end in a circle. Do not cut thread.

2. Embroider stripes around tail. Make 1¼" (3 cm) loops at tail tip. Cut ends of loops. Spread embroidery floss apart and apply a dab of glue to tail. Gather embroidery floss around dab of glue and trim tail into shape. Glue tail in place and sew to body, as shown in finished project diagram on page 61.

Make the hooves.

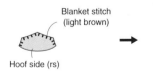

Blanket stitch
(light brown)

Hoof side (rs)

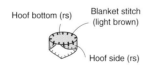

Hoof bottom (rs)

Blanket stitch
(light brown)

Hoof side (rs)

1. Blanket stitch along top of each **hoof side**.

2. Align each **hoof side** with a **hoof bottom** and sew.

3. Glue hooves to **soles**.

Materials

Adult Kangaroo

- Felt pieces
  - Brown: 8" x 8" (20 x 20 cm)
  - Beige: 2½" x 4" (6 x 10 cm)
  - Dark brown: ⅜" x ¾" (1 x 2 cm)
- Machine sewing thread in brown and beige
- 6-strand embroidery floss in dark brown
- 4¼" (11 cm) of 21-gauge plastic wire
- Two ⅛" (0.3 cm) diameter black eye buttons
- Polyester stuffing
- Quick-dry tacky glue

Joey

- Felt pieces
  - Brown: 1¼" x 2½" (3 x 6 cm)
- Machine sewing thread in brown
- 6-strand embroidery floss in dark brown
- Two ⅛" (0.3 cm) diameter black eye buttons
- Polyester stuffing
- Quick-dry tacky glue

Kangaroos
Shown on page 12

Cutting Instructions

Trace and cut out the following templates on pattern sheet A:

Adult Kangaroo

Beige Felt
- Body front (cut 1)
- Pouch lining (cut 1 for female kangaroo only)
- Ears (cut 2)

Brown Felt
- Body side (cut 2)
- Body top (cut 1)
- Ears (cut 2)

- Arms (cut 4)
- Legs (cut 4)
- Soles (cut 2)

Dark Brown Felt
- Eye pieces (cut 2)

Joey

Brown Felt
- Sides (cut 2)
- Top (cut 1)
- Ears (cut 2)

Finished Project

Male

Female

About 4" (10 cm) tall

About 4¼" (11 cm) long

Make the body.

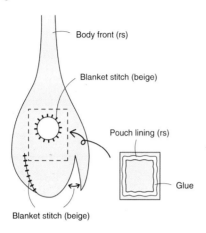

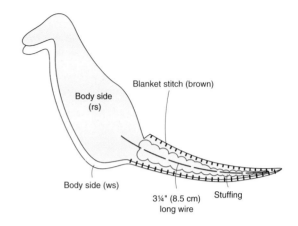

1. Align darts on **body front** and sew. For female kangaroo only, cut a hole in **body front**, as indicated on template. Blanket stitch around raw edge of hole. Apply glue to edges of **pouch lining**. Adhere **pouch** lining to wrong side of **body front** behind hole.

2. Sew two **body sides** together, inserting wire into tail and stuffing as you work.

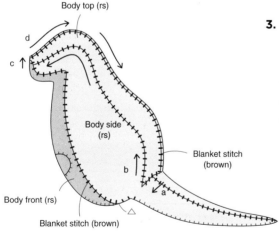

3. Align **body sides** with both **body top** and **body front** and sew, following direction indicated by arrows a-d in diagram. Align one **body side** with **body front** and sew. For male kangaroo, repeat for other **body side**. For female kangaroo, other **body side** will be attached later.

Make the joey (for the female kangaroo only).

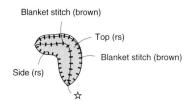

Blanket stitch (brown)
Top (rs)
Blanket stitch (brown)
Side (rs)
☆

Ear (rs)
Blanket stitch (brown)
Blanket stitch (brown)

1. Align one **side** with **top** and sew. Repeat for other **side**, stuffing as you work.

2. Blanket stitch around edges of each **ear.** Fold each ear in half inwardly and make two stitches at base, stitching through both edges, to secure fold.

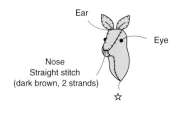

Ear
Eye
Nose
Straight stitch
(dark brown, 2 strands)
☆

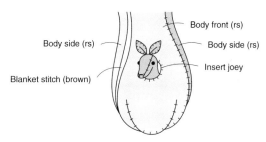

Body front (rs)
Body side (rs)
Body side (rs)
Insert joey
Blanket stitch (brown)

3. Sew **ears** to top of head. Embroider nose. Use a large needle to puncture holes in head at position to attach eyes. Insert eye buttons and glue to secure.

4. Apply glue to base of joey and insert into pouch. On female kangaroo, align open **body side** with **body front** and sew, stuffing as you work.

Finish the face.

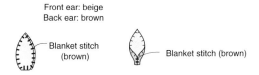

Front ear: beige
Back ear: brown
Blanket stitch
(brown)
Blanket stitch (brown)

1. For each **ear,** layer two colors of felt and sew together around all edges. Fold each ear in half inwardly and make two stitches at base, stitching through both edges, to secure fold.

Finish the face (continued).

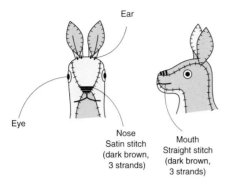

Ear

Eye

Nose
Satin stitch
(dark brown,
3 strands)

Mouth
Straight stitch
(dark brown,
3 strands)

2. Sew **ears** to top of head. Embroider nose and mouth. Hide knots at position to attach arms. Refer to page 40 to make and attach eyes.

Make the arms.

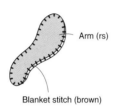

Arm (rs)

Blanket stitch (brown)

1. Sew two **arm** pieces together, stuffing, as you work. Repeat for other **arm**.

Make the legs.

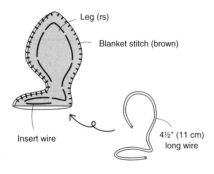

Leg (rs)

Blanket stitch (brown)

Insert wire

4½" (11 cm)
long wire

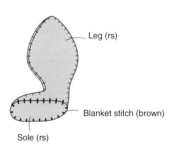

Leg (rs)

Blanket stitch (brown)

Sole (rs)

1. Sew two **leg** pieces together along half of leg. Do not cut thread. Bend wire into shape of leg and insert.

2. Stuff leg. Finish sewing leg together, leaving bottom edge open. Align **sole** with **leg** and sew. Repeat for other **leg**. Sew underside of **arms** and **legs** to body.

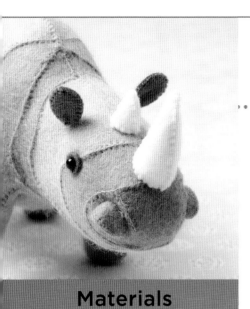

Rhinoceros Shown on page 14

Cutting Instructions

Trace and cut out the following templates on pattern sheet A:

Light Brown Felt
- A (cut 1)
- D (cut 1)
- G (cut 1)
- L (cut 1)
- Nostril side (cut 4)

Light Gray Felt
- B (cut 1)
- E (cut 2)
- H (cut 2)
- I (cut 1)
- K (cut 1)
- M (cut 1)
- Soles (cut 4)
- Ears (cut 2)

- Tail (cut 1)

Beige Felt
- C (cut 1)
- F (cut 2)
- J (cut 1)

Brown Felt
- Ears (cut 2)
- Nostril base (cut 2)
- Eye pieces (cut 2)

Off-White Felt
- Small horn (cut 2)
- Small horn bottom (cut 1)
- Large horn (cut 2)
- Large horn bottom (cut 1)

Materials

- Felt pieces
  - Light brown: 5½" x 6¾" (14 x 17 cm)
  - Light gray: 8" x 8" (20 x 20 cm)
  - Beige: 4" x 4" (10 x 10 cm)
  - Brown: ¾" x 1½" (2 x 4 cm)
  - Off-white: 2" x 2¾" (5 x 7 cm)
- Machine thread in light gray and off-white
- 6-strand embroidery floss in light gray
- 14½" (37 cm) of 21-gauge plastic wire
- Two ¼" (0.4 cm) diameter black eye buttons
- Polyester stuffing
- Quick-dry tacky glue

Finished Project

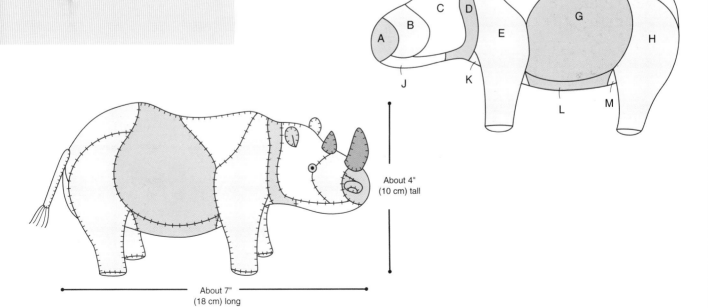

About 4" (10 cm) tall

About 7" (18 cm) long

Make the body.

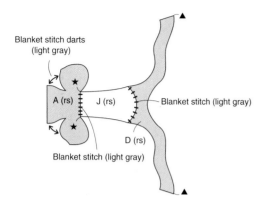

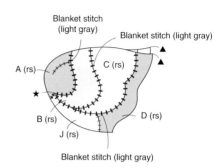

1. Align darts on **A** and sew. Align **A** with **J** (★) and sew. Align **J** with **D** and sew.

2. Align **A** with **B** and sew. Align **B** with **C** and sew. Align **ABC** with **JD** and sew.

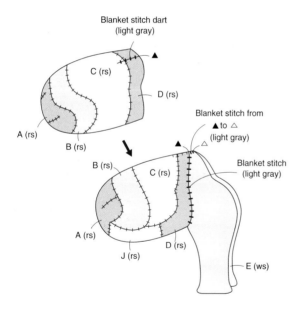

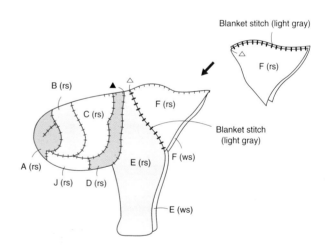

3. Align dart on **C** and **D** and sew. Align two **E** pieces and sew from ▲-△ using 2-3 stitches. Align **D** with one **E** piece and sew. Repeat with other **E** piece.

4. Align two **F** pieces and sew. Align one **E** with one **F** piece and sew. Repeat for other side.

Make the body (continued).

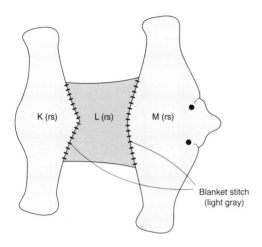

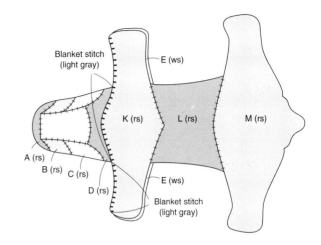

5. Align **K** with **L**, then **L** with **M** and sew.

6. Align **D** with **K** and sew. Align **E** with **K** and sew. Repeat for other side.

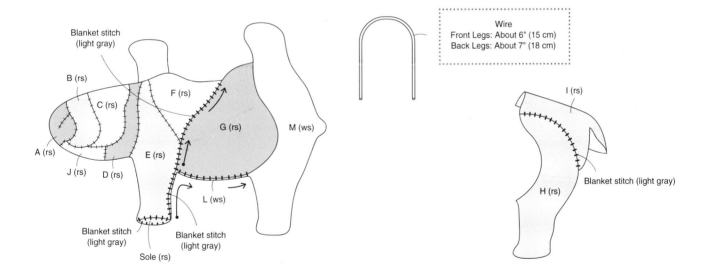

7. Align **E** with **K**, then **G** with **L** and sew. Repeat for other side. Align **E**, **K**, and one **sole** and sew. Repeat for other front leg. Align **E**, **F**, and **G** and sew. Repeat for other side, stuffing head as you work. Bend wires into two U-shaped pieces, as shown in diagram. Insert the 6" (15 cm) long wire into front legs and stuff.

8. Align **H** with **I** and sew. Repeat for other side.

Make the body (continued).

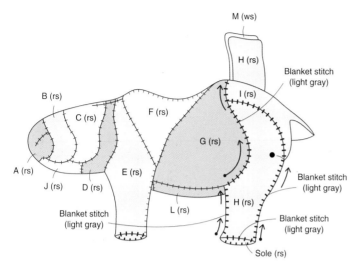

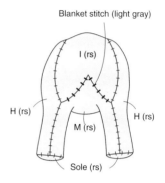

9. Align **H** with **M** and sew along inner back leg. Repeat for other side. Align **G**, **H**, and **I** and sew. Align **H** with **M** and sew along outer back leg. Repeat for other side. Align **H**, **M**, and one **sole** and sew. Repeat for other back leg.

10. Insert the 7" (18 cm) long wire into back legs and stuff. Stuff bottom and sew rhino closed along rear end.

Finish the face.

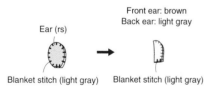

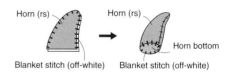

1. For each **ear**, layer two colors of felt and sew together around all edges. Fold each ear in half inwardly and make two stitches at base, stitching through both layers, to secure fold.

2. For each horn, sew two **horn** pieces together and stuff. Align each **horn** with a **horn bottom** and sew.

Finish the face (continued).

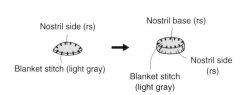

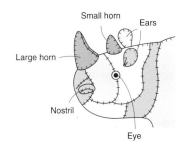

3. For each nostril, sew two **nostril side** pieces together. Align each **nostril side** with a **nostril base** piece and sew.

4. Sew **ears**, **horns**, and **nostrils** to head. Refer to page 40 to make and attach eyes.

Make the tail.

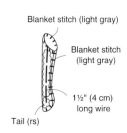

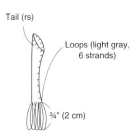

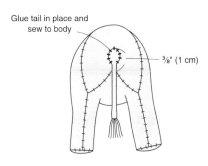

1. Fold **tail** in half widthwise and sew edges together, stuffing as you work. Insert wire. Add more stuffing. Leave end of tail open. This end will attach to body. Sew around end in a circle. Do not cut thread.

2. Make ¾" (2 cm) loops at tail tip. Cut ends of loops. Spread embroidery floss apart and apply a dab of glue to tail. Gather embroidery floss around dab of glue and trim tail into shape.

3. Glue tail in place and sew to body, about ⅜" (1 cm) from bottom seam.

Panda Shown on page 16

Cutting Instructions

Trace and cut out the following templates on pattern sheet A:

Off-White Felt
• Head front (cut 1)
• Muzzle (cut 1)
• Head back (cut 2)
• Lower body back (cut 2)
• Lower body front (cut 1)
• Tail bottom (cut 1)
• Tail top (cut 1)

Gray Felt
• Pad (cut 4)

Black Felt
• Eye patch (cut 2)
• Upper body (cut 2)
• Arm top (cut 2)
• Arm bottom (cut 2)
• Paw/sole (cut 4)
• Leg top (cut 2)
• Leg bottom (cut 2)
• Ears (cut 4)
• Nose (cut 2)

Materials

• Felt pieces
   - Off-white: 8" x 8" (20 x 20 cm)
   - Black: 8" x 8" (20 x 20 cm)
   - Gray: ¾" x ¾" (2 x 2 cm)
• Machine sewing thread in off-white and black
• 6-strand embroidery floss in beige and dark gray
• 9¾" (25 cm) of 21-gauge plastic wire
• Two ¼" (0.4 cm) diameter black eye buttons
• Polyester stuffing
• Quick-dry tacky glue

Finished Project

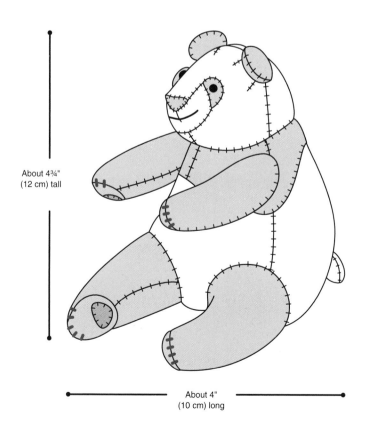

About 4¾"
(12 cm) tall

About 4"
(10 cm) long

Make the head.

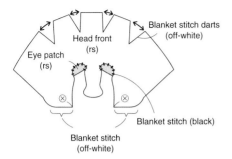

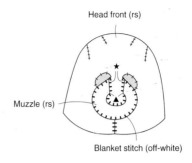

1. Layer **eye patches** on top of **head front** and sew. Align darts on **head front** and sew. Align two short edges of **head front** and sew.

2. Align **muzzle** with **head front** and sew.

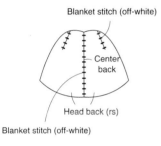

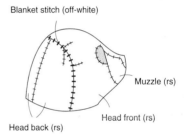

3. Align darts on **head back** and sew. Sew two head back pieces together.

4. Align **head front** with **head back** and sew.

Make the arms.

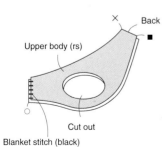

1. Sew two **upper body** pieces together (O).

Make the arms (continued).

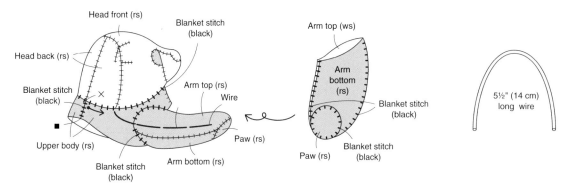

2. Align head with **upper body** (×) and sew. Sew **upper body** together along center back (■). Align an **arm top** with an **arm bottom** and sew. Align one **paw** with arm and sew. Align arm with **upper body** and sew. Repeat for other arm. Bend wire into a U-shape. Insert wire into arms and stuff.

Make the body.

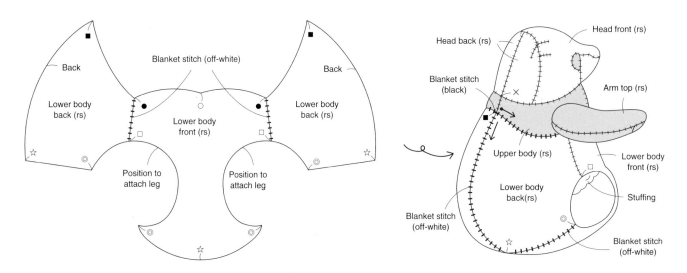

1. Align **lower body front** with **lower body back** pieces and sew.

2. Align **upper body** with lower body and sew. Sew two **lower body back** pieces together at center back. Align **lower body front** with **lower body back** along bottom (◎) and sew. Stuff body, stopping just above legs.

Make the legs.

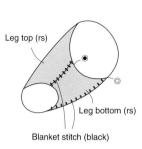

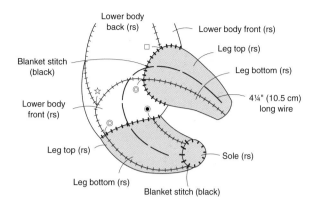

Leg top (rs)

Leg bottom (rs)

Blanket stitch (black)

Lower body back (rs)

Lower body front (rs)

Leg top (rs)

Leg bottom (rs)

Blanket stitch (black)

4¼" (10.5 cm) long wire

Lower body front (rs)

Leg top (rs)

Leg bottom (rs)

Sole (rs)

Blanket stitch (black)

1. Align a **leg top** with a **leg bottom** and sew. Repeat for other leg.

2. Align each leg with lower body and sew. Bend wire into a U-shape, insert into legs, and stuff. Align a **sole** with a leg and sew. Repeat for other leg.

Finish the face.

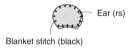

Ear (rs)

Blanket stitch (black)

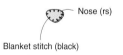

Nose (rs)

Blanket stitch (black)

1. For each ear, sew two **ear** pieces together around all edges, stuffing lightly as you work.

2. Sew two **nose** pieces together around all edges, stuffing lightly as you work.

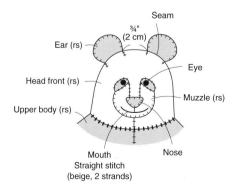

Seam

¾" (2 cm)

Ear (rs)

Eye

Head front (rs)

Muzzle (rs)

Upper body (rs)

Nose

Mouth
Straight stitch (beige, 2 strands)

3. Position **ears** about ¾" (2 cm) apart, just before seam on top of head, and sew. Puncture holes in head at position to attach eyes. Insert eye buttons and glue to secure. Embroider mouth. Hide knot at position to attach nose. Glue nose to head.

Make the tail.

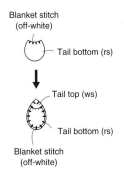

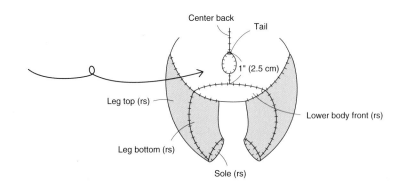

1. Blanket stitch along upper edge of **tail bottom**. Align **tail top** with **tail bottom** and sew, stuffing lightly as you work.

2. Sew tail to body about 1" (2.5 cm) from bottom seam.

Make the claws.

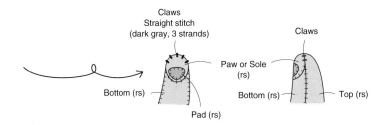

1. Blanket stitch around each **pad**.

2. Align each **pad** with each **paw** or **sole** and sew. Embroider claws.

Goat Shown on page 18

Materials

White Goat

- Felt pieces
  - Off-white: 6¼" x 8" (16 x 20 cm)
  - Golden yellow: 1¼" x 2½"
    (3 x 6 cm)
  - Pink: ¾" x 1¼" (2 x 3 cm)
- Machine thread in off-white and light brown
- 6-strand embroidery floss in beige and off-white
- 7½" (19 cm) of 21-gauge plastic wire
- Two ⅛" (0.3 cm) diameter black eye buttons
- Polyester stuffing
- Quick-dry tacky glue

Black Goat

- Felt pieces
  - Black: 6¼" x 8" (16 x 20 cm)
  - Light gray: 1¼" x 2½" (3 x 6 cm)
  - Beige: ⅜" x ¾" (1 x 2 cm)
  - Dark brown: ⅜" x ¾" (1 x 2 cm)
- Machine thread in dark gray and black
- 6-strand embroidery floss in dark gray and black
- 7½" (19 cm) of 21-gauge plastic wire
- Two ⅛" (0.3 cm) diameter black eye buttons
- Polyester stuffing
- Quick-dry tacky glue

Cutting Instructions

Trace and cut out the following templates on pattern sheet B:

White Goat

Off-White Felt
- Body bottom (cut 1)
- Body side (cut 2)
- Body top (cut 1)
- Tail (cut 1)
- Ears (cut 2)

Golden Yellow Felt
- Horns (cut 4)

Pink Felt
- Ears (cut 2)
- Eye pieces (cut 2)

Black Goat

Black Felt
- Body bottom (cut 1)
- Body side (cut 2)
- Body top (cut 1)
- Tail (cut 1)
- Ears (cut 2)

Light Gray Felt
- Horns (cut 4)

Beige Felt
- Ears (cut 2)

Dark Brown Felt
- Eye pieces (cut 2)

Finished Project

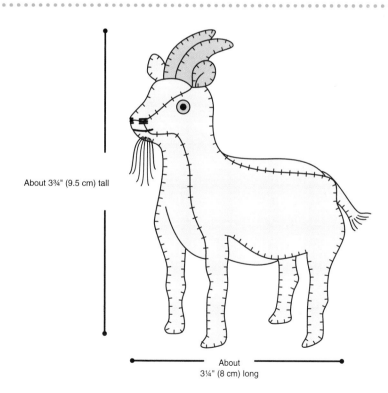

About 3¾" (9.5 cm) tall

About
3¼" (8 cm) long

Make the body.

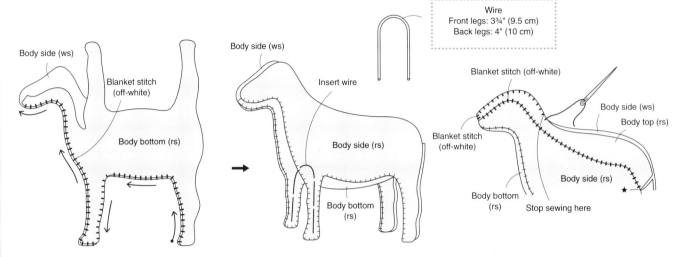

1. Align one **body side** with **body bottom** and sew. Repeat for other **body side**.

2. Bend wire into two U-shaped pieces. Insert the 3¾" (9.5 cm) long wire into front legs and stuff.

3. Align **body bottom** with **body top** and sew. Align one **body side** with **body top** and sew. On other side, sew **body side** and **body top** together along neck only. Do not cut thread. Stuff.

Embroider the nose and mouth.

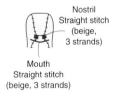

1. Embroider each nostril with three stitches. Embroider mouth. Hide knots in stuffing.

Finish the legs.

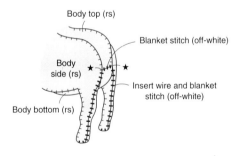

2. Align **body side** with **body bottom** and sew each leg. Insert stuffing and the 4" (10 cm) long wire as you work. Sew goat closed from neck to rear end (★).

Make the tail.

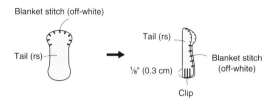

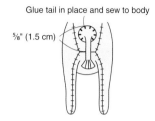

1. Blanket stitch around one end of **tail**. Fold **tail** in half widthwise and sew edges together, leaving ends open. Make ⅛" (0.3 cm) clips into other end of tail.

2. Glue **tail** in place and sew to body about ⅝" (1.5 cm) from bottom.

Finish the face.

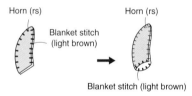

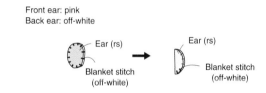

1. For each horn, sew two **horn** pieces together, leaving bottom open. Blanket stitch around bottom of each horn.

2. For each **ear**, layer two colors of felt and sew together around all edges. Fold each ear in half inwardly and sew across base to secure fold.

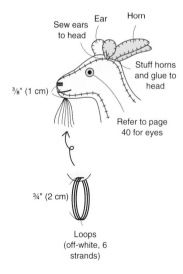

3. Sew **ears** to head. Stuff **horns** and glue to top of head. Refer to page 40 to make and attach eyes. Make three ¾" (2 cm) loops at chin. Cut ends of loops. Spread embroidery floss apart and apply a dab of glue to chin. Gather embroidery floss around dab of glue and trim beard into shape.

Sheep Shown on page 19

Cutting Instructions

Trace and cut out the following templates on pattern sheet B:

Off-White Felt
• Body side (cut 2)
• Body bottom (cut 1)
• Body top (cut 1)
• Ears (cut 2)
• Tail (cut 1)
• Tail base (cut 1)

Pink Felt
• Ears (cut 2)
• Eye pieces (cut 2)

Materials

• Felt pieces
  - Off-white: 6¼" x 7" (16 x 18 cm)
  - Pink: ¾" x ¾" (2 x 2 cm)
• Machine sewing thread in off-white
• 6-strand embroidery floss in light beige
• Variegated loop yarn in off-white/ beige
• 6" (15 cm) of 21-gauge plastic wire
• Two ⅛" (0.3 cm) diameter black eye buttons
• Polyester stuffing
• Quick-dry tacky glue

Finished Project

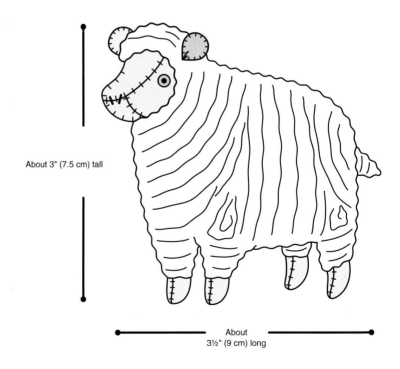

About 3" (7.5 cm) tall

About 3½" (9 cm) long

Make the body.

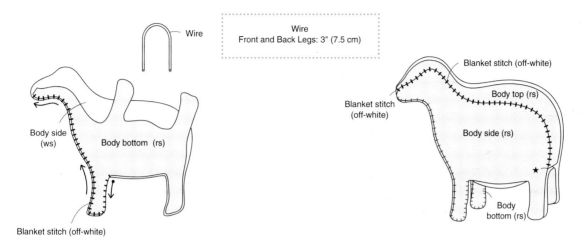

Wire

Wire
Front and Back Legs: 3" (7.5 cm)

Body side (ws)

Body bottom (rs)

Blanket stitch (off-white)

Blanket stitch (off-white)

Blanket stitch (off-white)

Body top (rs)

Body side (rs)

Body bottom (rs)

1. Align one **body side** with **body bottom** and sew from front leg to nose. Repeat for other **body side.** Bend wire into two U-shaped pieces. Insert one wire into front legs and stuff.

2. Align **body bottom** with **body top** and sew together along nose. Align one **body side** with **body top** and sew from nose to rear end. Repeat for other **body side**, stuffing as you work.

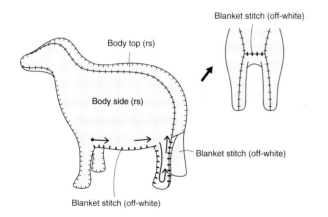

Blanket stitch (off-white)

Body top (rs)

Body side (rs)

Blanket stitch (off-white)

Blanket stitch (off-white)

3. Align one **body side** with **body bottom** and sew from stomach to back legs. Repeat for other **body side**, inserting remaining wire and stuffing as you work. Stuff bottom and sew sheep closed along rear end.

Finish the face.

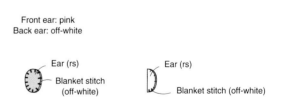

Front ear: pink
Back ear: off-white

Ear (rs)
Blanket stitch (off-white)

Ear (rs)
Blanket stitch (off-white)

1. For each **ear**, layer two colors of felt and sew together around all edges. Fold each ear in half and sew across base to secure fold.

Finish the face (continued).

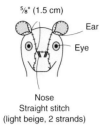

⅝" (1.5 cm)

Ear

Eye

Nose
Straight stitch
(light beige, 2 strands)

2. Sew **ears** to head. Refer to page 40 to make and attach eyes. Embroider nose with two straight stitches.

Make the tail.

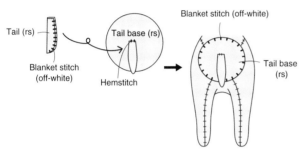

Tail (rs)

Blanket stitch
(off-white)

Tail base (rs)

Hemstitch

Blanket stitch (off-white)

Tail base
(rs)

1. Fold **tail** in half widthwise and sew edges together. Position **tail** on top of **tail base** so seam is not visible. Hemstitch **tail** to center of **tail base**. Sew **tail base** to body.

Make the wool.

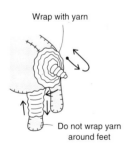

Wrap with yarn

Do not wrap yarn
around feet

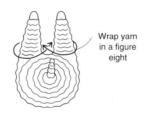

Wrap yarn
in a figure
eight

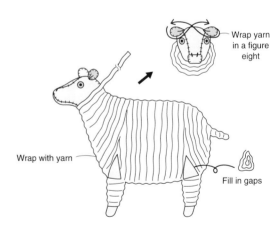

Wrap yarn
in a figure
eight

Wrap with yarn

Fill in gaps

1. Apply glue to **tail** and **tail base**. Wrap a short piece of yarn from **tail base** to tail tip. Wrap another short piece of yarn around **tail base**. Wrap yarn around each back leg. Do not wrap feet.

2. At top of back legs, wrap yarn in a figure eight shape to cover body.

3. Wrap yarn around body, front legs, and neck. At top of head, wrap yarn between ears in a figure eight shape. Fill in gaps at top of legs using short pieces of yarn. Tuck yarn ends underneath wrapped yarn and glue to secure.

Materials

- Felt pieces
  - Off-white: 8" x 8" (20 x 20 cm)
  - Black: 2½" x 4" (6 x 10 cm)
  - Pink: ¾" x 2" (2 x 5 cm)
  - Brown: ⅜" x ¾" (1 x 2 cm)
- Machine sewing thread in off-white, beige, and black
- 6-strand embroidery floss in off-white and beige
- 10¼" (26 cm) of 21-gauge plastic wire
- Two ⅛" (0.3 cm) diameter black eye buttons
- Polyester stuffing
- Quick-dry tacky glue

Cows: Calf Shown on page 20

Cutting Instructions

Trace and cut out the following templates on pattern sheet B:

Off-White Felt
- Body side (cut 2)
- Body bottom (cut 1)
- Body top (cut 1)
- Tail (cut 1)

Black Felt
- Spots (cut 2 of each)
- Ears (cut 2)

Pink Felt
- Nose (cut 1)
- Ears (cut 2)

Brown Felt
- Eye pieces (cut 2)

Finished Project

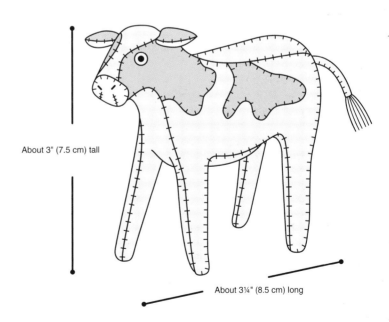

About 3" (7.5 cm) tall

About 3¼" (8.5 cm) long

Make the body.

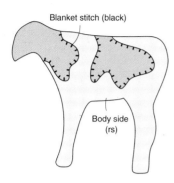

Blanket stitch (black)

Body side (rs)

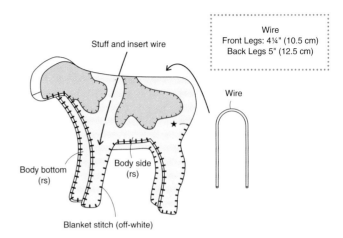

Wire
Front Legs: 4¼" (10.5 cm)
Back Legs: 5" (12.5 cm)

Stuff and insert wire

Wire

Body bottom (rs)

Body side (rs)

Blanket stitch (off-white)

1. Align spots on **body side** and sew. Repeat for other **body side**, making sure to create a symmetrical mirror image of first side.

2. Align one **body side** with **body bottom** and sew from nose to rear end. Repeat for other **body side**. Stuff feet. Bend wires into two U-shaped pieces, insert into legs, and stuff.

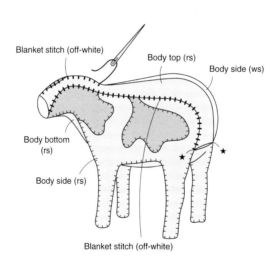

Blanket stitch (off-white)

Body top (rs)

Body side (ws)

Body bottom (rs)

Body side (rs)

Blanket stitch (off-white)

3. Align one **body side** with **body top** and sew. On other side, sew **body side** and **body top** together from nose to neck only. Do not cut thread.

Make the nose.

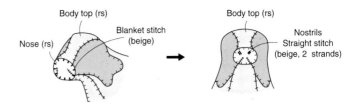

1. Align **nose** as indicated by arrows and sew.

2. Sew **nose** to head and stuff. Embroider nostrils with two straight stitches. Hide knots in stuffing.

Finish the body.

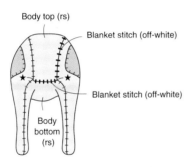

1. Stuff body. Align **body side** with **body top** (★) and sew. Stuff bottom and sew cow closed along rear end.

Finish the face.

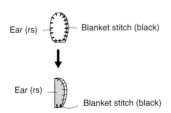

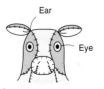

1. For each **ear**, layer two colors of felt and sew together around all edges. Fold each ear in half inwardly and sew across base to secure fold.

2. Sew **ears** to head. Refer to page 40 to make and attach eyes.

Make the tail.

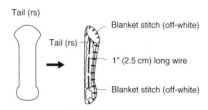

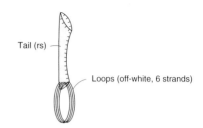

1. Fold **tail** in half widthwise and sew edges together, stuffing as you work. Insert wire. Leave end of tail open. This side will attach to body. Sew around tail in a circle. Do not cut thread.

2. Make loops at tail tip. Cut ends of loops. Spread embroidery floss apart and apply a dab of glue to tail. Gather embroidery floss around dab of glue and trim tail into shape.

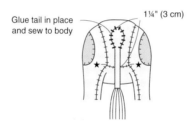

3. Glue tail in place and sew to body, about 1¼" (3 cm) from bottom.

Cows: Adult Shown on page 20

Cutting Instructions

Trace and cut out the following templates on pattern sheet B:

Off-White Felt
- Body side (cut 2)
- Body bottom (cut 1)
- Body top (cut 1)
- Tail (cut 1)
- Soles (cut 4)

Black Felt
- Spots (cut 2 of each)
- Ears (cut 2)

Pink Felt
- Nose (cut 1)
- Ears (cut 2)

- Udder center (cut 1)
- Udder base (cut 1)
- Udder sides (cut 2)

Brown Felt
- Eye pieces (cut 2)

Dark Beige Felt
- Hoof side (cut 4)
- Hoof bottom (cut 4)

Golden Yellow Felt
- Horns (cut 4)

Materials

- Felt pieces
  - Off-white: Two 8" x 8" (20 x 20 cm)
  - Black: 4" x 6" (10 x 15 cm)
  - Dark beige: 2" x 2½" (5 x 6 cm)
  - Pink: 2½" x 4" (6 x 10 cm)
  - Golden yellow: 1½" x 1½" (4 x 4 cm)
  - Brown: ⅜" x ¾" (1 x 2 cm)
- Machine sewing thread in off-white, beige, black, and light brown
- 6-strand embroidery floss in off-white and beige
- 13" (33 cm) of 21-gauge plastic wire
- Two ¼" (0.4 cm) diameter black eye buttons
- Polyester stuffing
- Quick-dry tacky glue

Finished Project

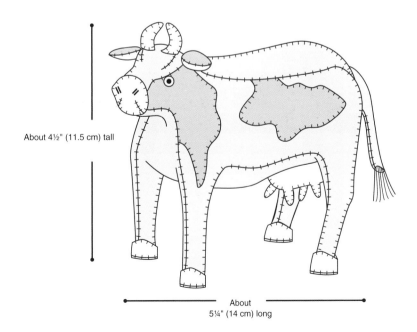

About 4½" (11.5 cm) tall

About
5¼" (14 cm) long

Make the body.

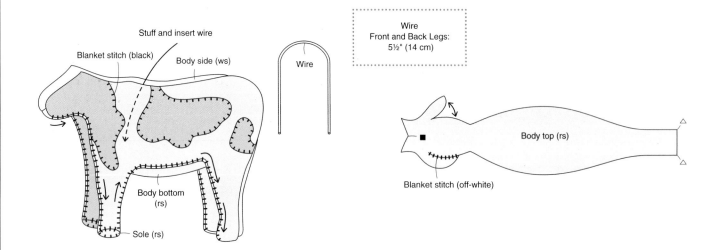

1. Align spots on **body side** and sew. Repeat for other **body side**, making sure to create a symmetrical mirror image of first side. Align one **body side** with **body bottom** and sew from nose to inner back legs. Repeat for other **body side**. Sew **soles** to front legs. Bend wire into two U-shaped pieces. Stuff front feet. Insert one plastic wire. Stuff front legs.

2. Align **body top** darts, as indicated by arrows and sew.

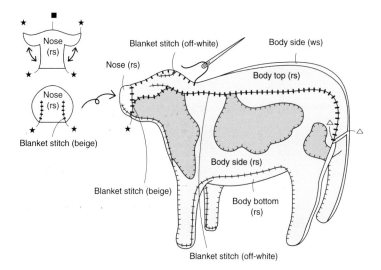

3. Align one **body side** with **body top** and sew. On other side, sew **body side** and **body top** together from nose to neck only. Do not cut thread. Align **nose**, as indicated by arrows and sew. Sew **nose** to head. Stuff head.

Make the body (continued).

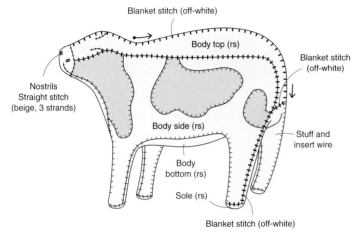

Blanket stitch (off-white)

Body top (rs)

Blanket stitch (off-white)

Nostrils
Straight stitch
(beige, 3 strands)

Body side (rs)

Stuff and
insert wire

Body
bottom (rs)

Sole (rs)

Blanket stitch (off-white)

4. Embroider nostrils with two straight stitches each. Hide knot in stuffing. Sew outer back legs together. Sew **soles** to back legs. Stuff back feet. Insert other wire. Stuff back legs and body. Align **body side** with **body top** and sew. Stuff bottom and sew cow closed along rear end.

Make the udders.

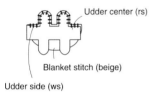

Udder center (rs)

Blanket stitch (beige)

Udder side (ws)

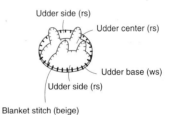

Udder side (rs)

Udder center (rs)

Udder base (ws)

Udder side (rs)

Blanket stitch (beige)

1. Align **udder center** with one **udder side** and sew. Repeat for other **udder side**.

2. Align udder with **udder base** and sew, stuffing as you work. Sew udder to **body bottom**.

Finish the face.

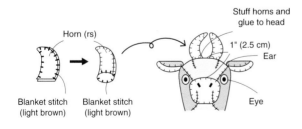

Horn (rs)

Stuff horns and
glue to head

1" (2.5 cm)

Ear

Eye

Blanket stitch
(light brown)

Blanket stitch
(light brown)

1. For each horn, sew two **horn** pieces together. Leaving bottom of each horn open, sew around edge. Stuff horns and glue to head. Make **ears**, as shown on page 87, and sew ears to head. Refer to page 40 to make and attach eyes. To finish the cow, refer to page 55 to make hooves and page 88 to make tail.

Materials

Pink Pig

- Felt pieces
  - Pink: 4" x 8" (10 x 20 cm)
  - Beige: ¾" x 1½" (2 x 4 cm)
  - Dark beige: ⅜" x ¾" (1 x 2 cm)
- Machine sewing thread in light beige

Brown Pig

- Felt pieces
  - Reddish brown: 4" x 8" (10 x 20 cm)
  - Pink: ¾" x 1¼" (2 x 3 cm)
  - Brown: ⅜" x ¾" (1 x 2 cm)
  - Light brown: ⅜" x ⅝" (1 x 1.5 cm)
- Machine sewing thread in brown

For Both Pigs

- 6-strand embroidery floss in light brown
- 6¾" (17 cm) of 21-gauge plastic wire
- Two ⅛" (0.3 cm) diameter black eye buttons
- Polyester stuffing
- Quick-dry tacky glue

$\mathcal{P}$ig Shown on page 22

Cutting Instructions

Trace and cut out the following templates on pattern sheet B:

Pink Pig

Pink Felt
- Body side (cut 2)
- Body bottom (cut 1)
- Body top (cut 1)
- Ears (cut 2)
- Tail (cut 1)

Beige Felt
- Nose (cut 1)
- Ears (cut 2)

Dark Beige Felt
- Eye pieces (cut 2)

Brown Pig

Reddish Brown Felt
- Body side (cut 2)
- Body bottom (cut 1)
- Body top (cut 1)
- Ears (cut 2)
- Tail (cut 1)

Pink Felt
- Ears (cut 2)

Brown Felt
- Eye pieces (cut 2)

Light Brown Felt
- Nose (cut 1)

Finished Project

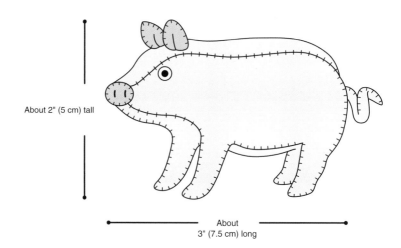

About 2" (5 cm) tall

About 3" (7.5 cm) long

Make the body.

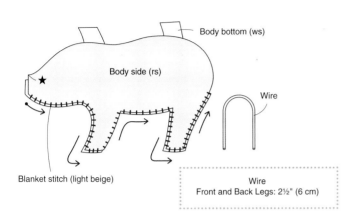

Body bottom (ws)

Body side (rs)

Wire

Blanket stitch (light beige)

Wire
Front and Back Legs: 2½" (6 cm)

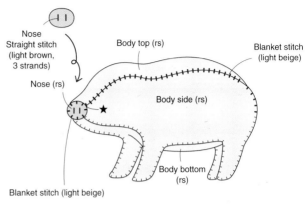

Nose
Straight stitch
(light brown,
3 strands)

Body top (rs)

Blanket stitch
(light beige)

Nose (rs)

Body side (rs)

Body bottom
(rs)

Blanket stitch (light beige)

1. Align one **body side** with **body bottom** and sew. Repeat for other **body side**. Bend wire into two U-shaped pieces. Stuff feet. Insert wires into legs and stuff.

2. Align one **body side** with **body top** and sew. On other side, sew pieces together along nose only, using 3-4 stitches. Do not cut thread. Embroider **nose** with two straight stitches. Sew **nose** to head. Align remaining **body side** with **body top** and sew from nose to rear end, stuffing as you work.

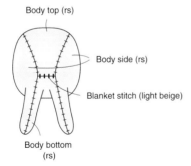

Body top (rs)

Body side (rs)

Blanket stitch (light beige)

Body bottom
(rs)

3. Stuff bottom and sew pig closed along rear end.

Make the face.

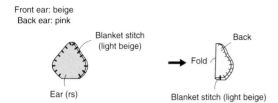

Front ear: beige
Back ear: pink

Blanket stitch (light beige)

Ear (rs)

Fold

Back

Blanket stitch (light beige)

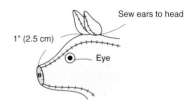

Sew ears to head

1" (2.5 cm)

Eye

1. For each **ear**, layer two colors of felt and sew together around all edges. Fold each ear in half inwardly and sew one stitch across bottom to secure the fold.

2. Position ears on top of head, so they lean forward slightly, and sew. Refer to page 40 to make and attach eyes.

Make the tail.

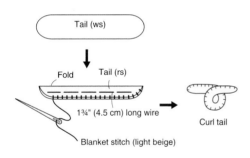

Tail (ws)

Fold

Tail (rs)

1¾" (4.5 cm) long wire

Blanket stitch (light beige)

Curl tail

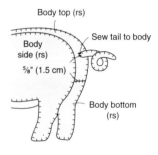

Body top (rs)

Sew tail to body

Body side (rs)

⅝" (1.5 cm)

Body bottom (rs)

1. Fold **tail** in half and sew edges together, inserting wire as you work. Curl tail.

2. Sew tail to body, about ⅝" (1.5 cm) from bottom.

Materials

Brown Rabbit

- Felt pieces
  - Light brown: 4" x 4¾" (10 x 12 cm)
  - Beige: 2½" x 3" (6 x 7.5 cm)
  - Brown: ⅜" x ¾" (1 x 2 cm)
  - Pink: ¾" x 1" (2 x 2.5 cm)
- Machine sewing thread in brown
- 6-strand embroidery floss in khaki

Gray Rabbit

- Felt pieces
  - Light gray: 4" x 4¾" (10 x 12 cm)
  - Off-white: 2½" x 3" (6 x 7.5 cm)
  - Beige: ⅜" x ¾" (1 x 2 cm)
  - Pink: ¾" x 1" (2 x 2.5 cm)
- Machine sewing thread in gray
- 6-strand embroidery floss in gray

Beige Rabbit

- Felt pieces
  - Beige: 4" x 4¾" (10 x 12 cm)
  - Off-white: 2½" x 3" (6 x 7.5 cm)
  - Light brown: ⅜" x ¾" (1 x 2 cm)
  - Pink: ¾" x 1" (2 x 2.5 cm)
- Machine sewing thread in beige
- 6-strand embroidery floss in light brown

For All Rabbits

- 8¼" (21 cm) of 21-gauge plastic wire
- Two ⅛" (0.3 cm) diameter black eye buttons
- Polyester stuffing
- Quick-dry tacky glue

Rabbit

Shown on page 23

Cutting Instructions

Trace and cut out the following templates on pattern sheet B:

Brown Rabbit

Light Brown Felt
- Body side (cut 2)
- Head top (cut 1)
- Ears (cut 2)
- Legs (cut 4)
- Soles (cut 2)
- Tail sides (cut 2)
- Tail bottom (cut 1)

Beige Felt
- Body front (cut 1)

Brown Felt
- Eye pieces (cut 2)

Pink Felt
- Ears (cut 2)

Gray Rabbit

Light Gray Felt
- Body side (cut 2)
- Head top (cut 1)
- Ears (cut 2)
- Legs (cut 4)
- Soles (cut 2)
- Tail sides (cut 2)
- Tail bottom (cut 1)

Off-White Felt
- Body front (cut 1)

Beige Felt
- Eye pieces (cut 2)

Pink Felt
- Ears (cut 2)

Beige Rabbit

Beige Felt
- Body side (cut 2)
- Head top (cut 1)
- Ears (cut 2)
- Legs (cut 4)
- Soles (cut 2)
- Tail sides (cut 2)
- Tail bottom (cut 1)

Off-White Felt
- Body front (cut 1)

Light Brown Felt
- Eye pieces (cut 2)

Pink Felt
- Ears (cut 2)

Finished Project

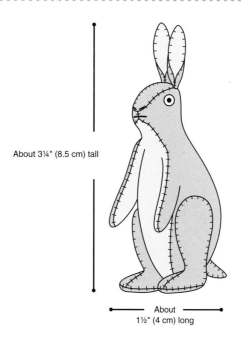

About 3¼" (8.5 cm) tall

About 1½" (4 cm) long

Make the body.

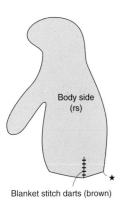

Body side (rs)

Blanket stitch darts (brown)

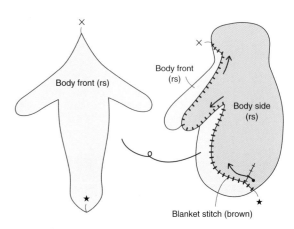

Body front (rs)

Body front (rs)

Body side (rs)

Blanket stitch (brown)

1. Align **body side** darts and sew. Repeat for other **body side**.

2. Align one **body side** with **body front** and sew. Repeat for other **body side**.

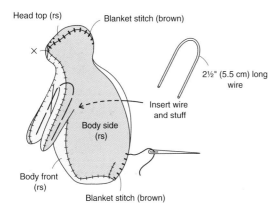

Head top (rs)   Blanket stitch (brown)

2½" (5.5 cm) long wire

Insert wire and stuff

Body side (rs)

Body front (rs)

Blanket stitch (brown)

3. Align **head top** with one **body side** and sew. Repeat for other **body side**. Bend wire into a U-shape and insert into arms. Stuff arms and body. Sew two **body side** pieces together along back.

Make the face.

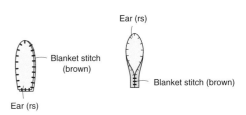

Ear (rs)

Blanket stitch (brown)

Ear (rs)

Blanket stitch (brown)

1. For each **ear**, layer two colors of felt and sew together around all edges. Fold each ear in half inwardly and make a few stitches at base, stitching through both edges to secure fold.

Make the face (continued).

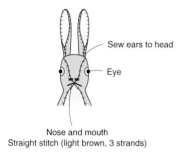

Sew ears to head

Eye

Nose and mouth
Straight stitch (light brown, 3 strands)

2. Position **ears** on top of head so they face outward and sew. Refer to page 40 to make and attach eyes. Embroider nose and mouth. Hide knots at position to attach leg.

Make the tail.

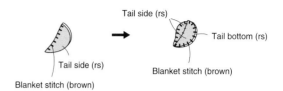

Tail side (rs)

Tail side (rs)

Tail bottom (rs)

Blanket stitch (brown)

Blanket stitch (brown)

1. Sew two **tail sides** together along straight edge. Align **tail bottom** with **tail sides** and sew, stuffing as you work.

Make the legs.

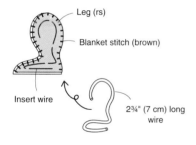

Leg (rs)

Blanket stitch (brown)

Insert wire

2¾" (7 cm) long wire

1. Sew two **leg** pieces together, leaving bottom open. Bend wire into shape of leg and insert. Repeat for other **leg**.

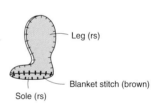

Leg (rs)

Blanket stitch (brown)

Sole (rs)

2. Stuff leg. Align **sole** with **leg** and sew. Repeat for other **leg**.

Finish the rabbit.

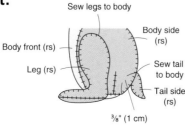

Sew legs to body

Body side (rs)

Body front (rs)

Sew tail to body

Leg (rs)

Tail side (rs)

⅜" (1 cm)

1. Position **legs** on **body sides** so soles align with rabbit bottom and sew underside of legs to body sides. Sew tail to rabbit about ⅜" (1 cm) from bottom.

Dogs: Pug

Shown on page 24

Cutting Instructions

Trace and cut out the following templates on pattern sheet B:

Beige Felt
- Head (cut 1)
- Body side (cut 2)
- Body bottom (cut 1)
- Body top (cut 1)
- Tail (cut 2)

Black Felt
- Face (cut 1)
- Mouth (cut 2)
- Ears (cut 4)

Dark Brown Felt
- Eye pieces (cut 2)

Finished Project

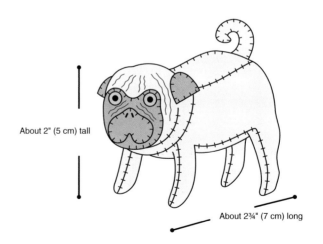

About 2" (5 cm) tall

About 2¾" (7 cm) long

Materials

- Felt pieces
  - Beige: 4¾" x 5½" (12 x 14 cm)
  - Black: 2" x 2" (5 x 5 cm)
  - Dark brown: ⅜" x ¾" (1 x 2 cm)
- Machine thread in beige and black
- 6-strand embroidery floss in dark gray
- 8" (20 cm) of 21-gauge plastic wire
- Two ⅛" (0.3 cm) diameter black eye buttons
- Polyester stuffing
- Quick-dry tacky glue

Make the head.

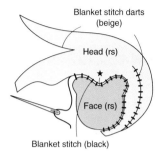

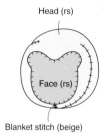

1. Align **head** darts and sew. Align **face** with **head** (★) and sew.

2. Sew **head** edges at chin.

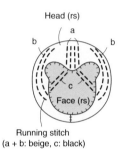

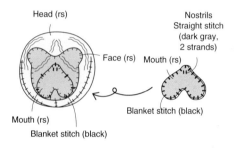

3. Pinch **head** and **face** to make wrinkles and sew using running stitches. Use beige thread for a and b wrinkles and black thread for c wrinkles.

4. Sew two **mouth** pieces together, stuffing as you work. Embroider nostrils. Sew **mouth** to **face**.

Make the body.

1. Align one **body side** with **body bottom** and sew. Repeat for other **body side**. Bend two wires into U-shaped pieces. Insert wires into legs and stuff.

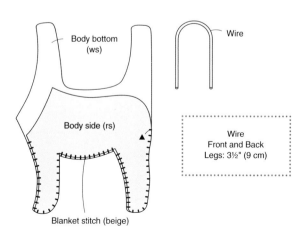

Make the body (continued).

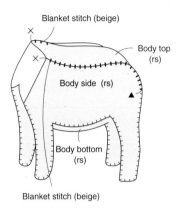

Blanket stitch (beige)

Body top (rs)

Body side (rs)

Body bottom (rs)

Blanket stitch (beige)

2. Align one **body side** with **body top** and sew. On other side, sew pieces together for 3-4 stitches only. Do not cut thread.

Attach the head and body.

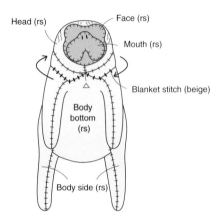

Head (rs)

Face (rs)

Mouth (rs)

Blanket stitch (beige)

Body bottom (rs)

Body side (rs)

1. Align **head** with body (△) and sew together around neck. Align **body side** with **body top** and sew to rear end, stuffing as you work.

Make the tail.

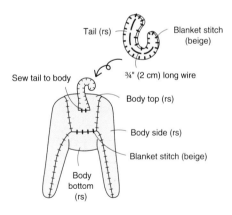

Tail (rs)

Blanket stitch (beige)

¾" (2 cm) long wire

Sew tail to body

Body top (rs)

Body side (rs)

Blanket stitch (beige)

Body bottom (rs)

1. Stuff bottom and sew pug closed along rear end. Sew two **tail** pieces together, inserting wire and stuffing as you work. Sew tail to body.

Finish the face.

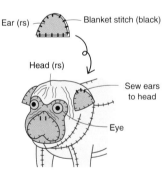

Ear (rs)

Blanket stitch (black)

Head (rs)

Sew ears to head

Eye

1. For each ear, sew two **ear** pieces together around all edges. Sew ears to head. Refer to page 40 to make and attach eyes.

Dogs: Shiba Shown on page 24

Cutting Instructions

Trace and cut out the following templates on pattern sheet B:

Tan Felt
- Body side (cut 2)
- Head top (cut 1)
- Head back (cut 2)
- Ears (cut 2)
- Tail (cut 1)

Off-White Felt
- Body bottom (cut 1)
- Head bottom (cut 1)
- Ears (cut 2)
- Tail (cut 1)

Black Felt
- Eye pieces (cut 2)

Finished Project

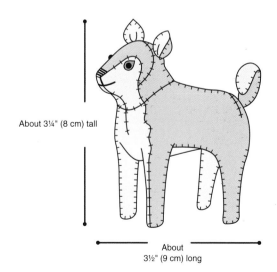

About 3¼" (8 cm) tall

About 3½" (9 cm) long

Materials

- Felt pieces
  - Tan: 4" x 6¾" (10 x 17 cm)
  - Off-white: 4" x 5½" (10 x 14 cm)
  - Black: ⅜" x ¾" (1 x 2 cm)
- Machine sewing thread in beige and off-white
- 6-strand embroidery floss in black
- 8¾" (22 cm) of 21-gauge plastic wire
- Two ⅛" (0.3 cm) diameter black eye buttons
- Polyester stuffing
- Quick-dry tacky glue

Make the body.

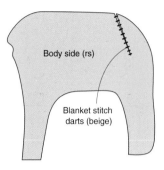

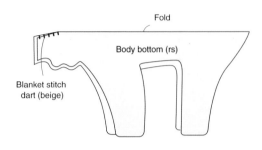

1. Align **body side** darts and sew. Repeat for other **body side**, making sure to make a symmetrical mirror image of first side.

2. Align **body bottom** darts and sew.

Make the head.

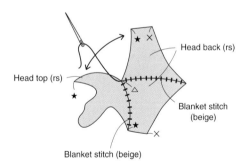

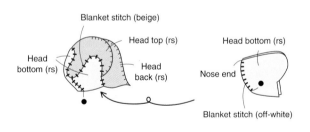

1. Sew two **head back** pieces together (△). Align **head top** with **head back** (★) and sew.

2. Sew two **head bottom** pieces together from nose to neck (●). Align **head bottom** with **head top** and sew.

Attach the head and body.

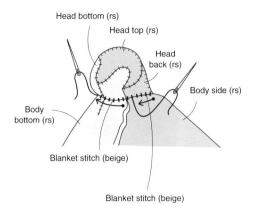

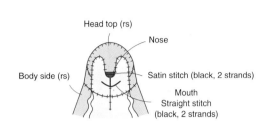

1. Align **head bottom** with **body bottom** and sew. Align **head back** with one **body side** and sew. Repeat for other **body side**.

2. Stuff head. Embroider nose and mouth.

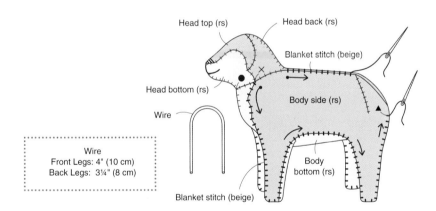

Wire
Front Legs: 4" (10 cm)
Back Legs: 3¼" (8 cm)

3. Bend wire into two U-shaped pieces. Align one **body side** with **body bottom** and sew, inserting wires into legs and stuffing as you work. Repeat for other **body side**. Sew two **body sides** together along back, stuffing as you work.

Finish the face.

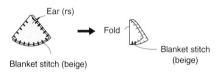

1. For each **ear**, layer two colors of felt and sew together around all edges. Fold each ear in half inwardly and sew across base using two stitches to secure fold.

2. Position ears so they face forward and sew them to **head back**, about ¼" (0.5 cm) apart. Refer to page 40 to make and attach eyes, cutting felt into a teardrop shape.

Make the tail.

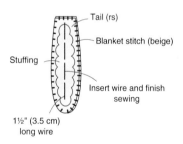

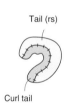

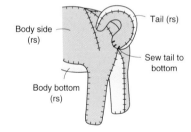

1. Sew two **tail** pieces together halfway around tail. Insert wire, stuff, and sew tail closed.

2. Curl tail so beige felt is on inside.

3. Sew tail to bottom.

Cats: Black

Shown on page 25

Materials

- Felt pieces
  - Black: 6" x 8" (15 x 20 cm)
  - Dark gray: ¾" x 1¼" (2 x 3 cm)
  - Yellow: ⅜" x ¾" (1 x 2 cm)
- Machine sewing thread in black
- 6-strand embroidery floss in dark gray
- 11¾" (30 cm) of 21-gauge plastic wire
- Two ⅛" (0.3 cm) diameter black eye buttons
- Polyester stuffing
- Quick-dry tacky glue

Cutting Instructions

Trace and cut out the following templates on pattern sheet B:

Black Felt
- Left body side (cut 1)
- Right body side (cut 1)
- Body front (cut 1)
- Head (cut 1)
- Ears (cut 2)
- Legs (cut 4)
- Soles (cut 2)
- Tail (cut 2)

Dark Gray Felt
- Ears (cut 2)

Yellow Felt
- Eye pieces (cut 2)

Finished Project

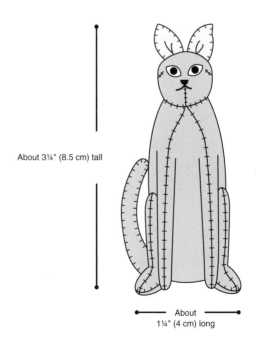

About 3¼" (8.5 cm) tall

About 1¼" (4 cm) long

Make the head and body.

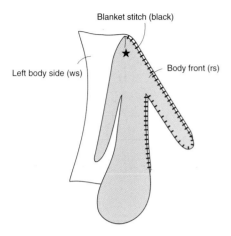

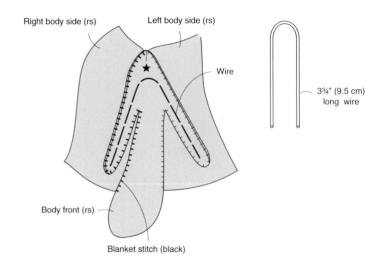

1. Align **body front** with **left body side** and sew.

2. Align **body front** with **right body side** and sew. Bend a 3¾" (9.5 cm) long wire into a U-shape. Insert wire into front legs and stuff.

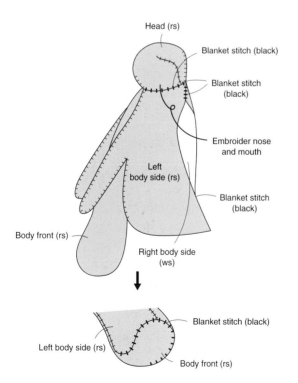

3. Refer to page 109 to sew head. Align head with body and sew. Sew **left and right body sides** together along back for 4-5 stitches only. Stuff head. Refer to page 110 to embroider nose and mouth and page 40 to make and attach eyes. Sew **left and right body sides** together along entire back. Stuff body. Align **body front** with **body sides** along bottom and sew.

Make the legs.

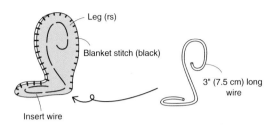

Leg (rs)
Blanket stitch (black)
3" (7.5 cm) long wire
Insert wire

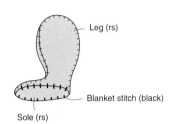

Leg (rs)
Blanket stitch (black)
Sole (rs)

1. Sew two **leg** pieces together, leaving bottom open. Bend a 3" (7.5 cm) long wire into shape of leg. Insert wire into leg. Repeat for other leg.

2. Stuff leg. Align sole with leg and sew. Repeat for the other leg.

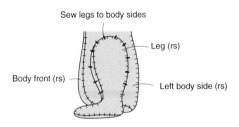

Sew legs to body sides
Leg (rs)
Body front (rs)
Left body side (rs)

3. Sew underside of **legs** to **body sides** so soles align with bottom of cat.

Make the tail.

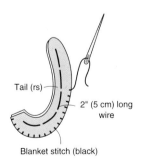

Tail (rs)
2" (5 cm) long wire
Blanket stitch (black)

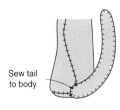

Sew tail to body

1. Sew two tail pieces together, inserting a 2" (5 cm) long wire and stuffing as you work.

2. Sew tail to back of cat.

Cats: Beige Shown on page 25

Cutting Instructions

Trace and cut out the following templates on pattern sheet B:

Beige Felt
- Head (cut 1)
- Body side (cut 2)
- Body bottom (cut 1)
- Body top (cut 1)
- Ears (cut 2)
- Tail (cut 1)

Pink Felt
- Ears (cut 2)

Dark Gray Felt
- Eye pieces (cut 2)

Materials

- Felt pieces
  - Beige: 6" x 8" (15 x 20 cm)
  - Pink: ¾" x 1¼" (2 x 3 cm)
  - Dark gray: ⅜" x ¾" (1 x 2 cm)
- Machine sewing thread in beige
- 6-strand embroidery floss in light brown
- 8¼" (21 cm) of 21-gauge plastic wire
- Two ⅛" (0.3 cm) diameter black eye buttons
- Polyester stuffing
- Quick-dry tacky glue

Finished Project

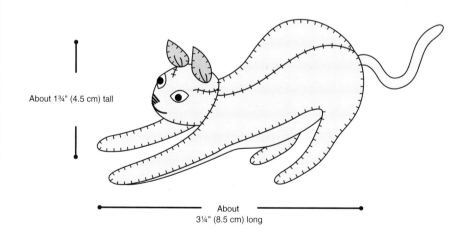

About 1¾" (4.5 cm) tall

About 3¼" (8.5 cm) long

Make the head.

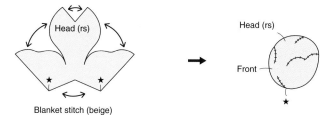

Blanket stitch (beige)

1. Align **head** darts as indicated by arrows and sew.

Make the body.

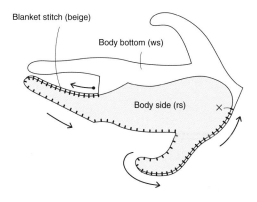

1. Align one **body side** with **body bottom** and sew from inner front leg to rear end. Repeat for other **body side**.

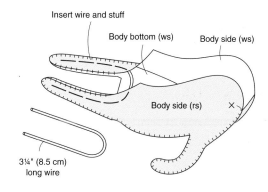

2. Bend two wires into U-shaped pieces. Lightly stuff paws. Insert wires and stuff front and back legs.

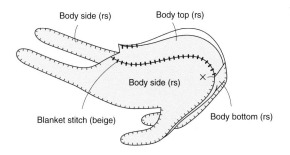

3. Align one **body side** with **body top** and sew. On other side, sew pieces together for 4-5 stitches only. Do not cut thread.

Attach the head and body.

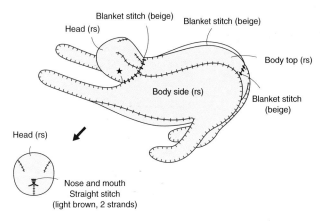

Blanket stitch (beige)
Head (rs)
Blanket stitch (beige)
Blanket stitch (beige)
Body top (rs)
Body side (rs)
Blanket stitch (beige)
Head (rs)
Nose and mouth
Straight stitch
(light brown, 2 strands)

1. Align head with body and sew. Stuff head. Embroider nose and mouth. Stuff body. Align **body side** with **body top** and sew to rear end. Stuff bottom and sew cat closed along rear end.

Finish the face.

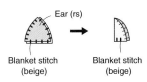

Ear (rs)
Blanket stitch (beige)
Blanket stitch (beige)

1. For each **ear**, layer two colors of felt and sew together around all edges. Fold each ear in half inwardly and sew across base using two stitches to secure fold.

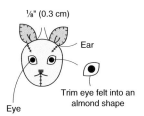

⅛" (0.3 cm)
Ear
Trim eye felt into an almond shape
Eye

2. Sew ears to head about ⅛" (0.3 cm) apart. Refer to page 40 to make and attach eyes, cutting felt into an almond shape.

Make the tail.

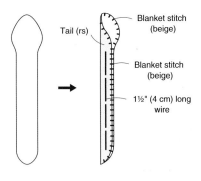

Tail (rs)
Blanket stitch (beige)
Blanket stitch (beige)
1½" (4 cm) long wire

1. Fold **tail** in half widthwise and sew edges together. Leave end of tail open. This side will attach to body. Sew around end in a circle. Do not cut thread. Insert wire into tail and stuff.

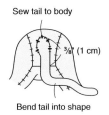

Sew tail to body
⅜" (1 cm)
Bend tail into shape

2. Sew tail to body, about ⅜" (1 cm) from bottom. Bend tail into shape.

Penguin

Shown on page 26

Materials

- Felt pieces
  - Black: 4" x 6" (10 x 15 cm)
  - Dark gray: 2¾" x 4" (7 x 10 cm)
  - Off-white: 2¾" x 4" (7 x 10 cm)
  - Golden yellow: 1¼" x 2½" (3 x 6 cm)
  - Red: ⅜" x ¾" (1 x 2 cm)
- Machine thread in off-white, black, light brown, and gray
- 13¾" (35 cm) of 21-gauge plastic wire
- Two ⅛" (0.3 cm) diameter black eye buttons
- Cardboard: ¾" x 1½" (2 x 4 cm)
- Polyester stuffing
- Quick-dry tacky glue

Cutting Instructions

Trace and cut out the following templates on pattern sheet B:

Black Felt
- Head (cut 2)
- Beak top (cut 1)
- Feet (cut 4)
- Wings (cut 2)

Dark Gray Felt
- Body side (cut 2)
- Bottom body back (cut 1)

Off-White Felt
- Body front (cut 1)
- Bottom body front (cut 1)
- Wings (cut 2)

Golden Yellow Felt
- Head side (cut 2)
- Beak bottom (cut 2)

Red Felt
- Eye pieces (cut 2)

Cardboard
- Foot (cut 2)

Finished Project

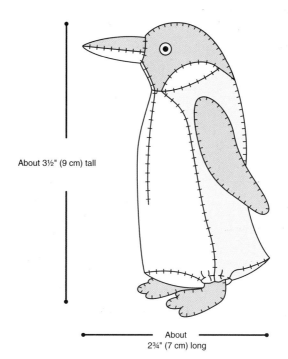

About 3½" (9 cm) tall

About
2¾" (7 cm) long

Make the head.

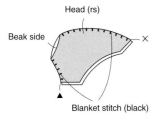

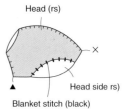

1. Sew two **head** pieces together.

2. Align head with one **head side** and sew. Repeat for the other **head side**.

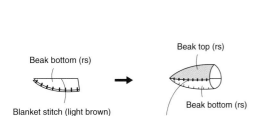

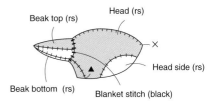

3. Sew two **beak bottom** pieces together. Align **beak top** with **beak bottom** and sew together along both sides.

4. Align head with beak and sew. Stuff beak.

Make the body.

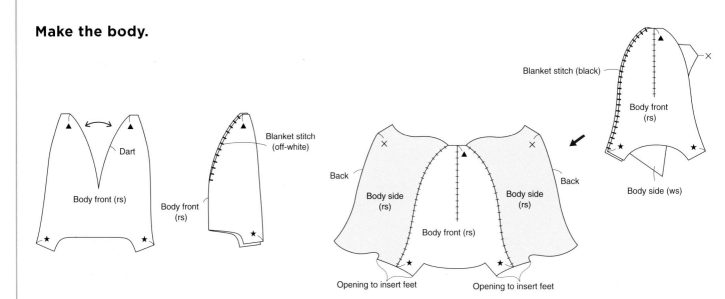

1. Align **body front** darts, as indicated by arrows and sew.

2. Align **body front** with one **body side** and sew. Repeat for other **body side**.

Attach the head and body.

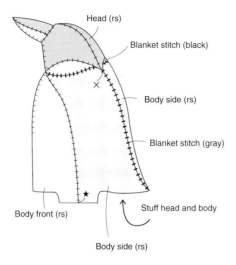

Head (rs)

Blanket stitch (black)

Body side (rs)

Blanket stitch (gray)

Body front (rs)

Stuff head and body

Body side (rs)

1. Align head with body (×) and sew together around neck. Sew **body sides** together along back. Stuff head and body.

Finish the body.

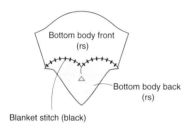

Bottom body front (rs)

Bottom body back (rs)

Blanket stitch (black)

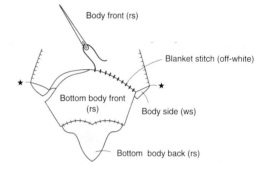

Body front (rs)

Blanket stitch (off-white)

Bottom body front (rs)

Body side (ws)

Bottom body back (rs)

1. Align **bottom body front** with **bottom body back** (△) and sew.

2. Align **body front** with **bottom body front** and sew.

Make the feet.

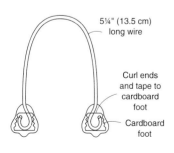

5¼" (13.5 cm) long wire

Curl ends and tape to cardboard foot

Cardboard foot

1. Bend plastic wire into a U-shape and curl both ends. Tape each end to a **cardboard foot**.

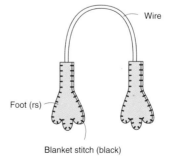

Wire

Foot (rs)

Blanket stitch (black)

2. For each foot, align two **foot** pieces with a **cardboard foot** sandwiched in between. Sew, stuffing as you work.

Attach the feet.

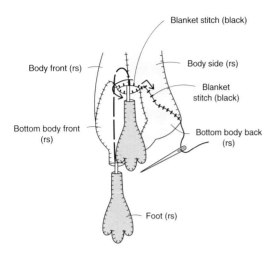

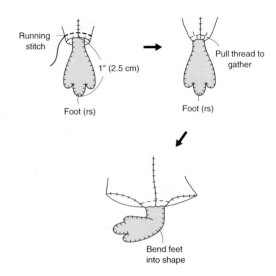

1. Insert feet into body and sew around opening at penguin bottom. Align **body sides** with **bottom body back** and sew, stuffing as you work.

2. Adjust each foot so it is about 1" (2.5 cm) long and secure with a running stitch around opening. Pull thread to gather and stitch to secure. Bend feet into shape.

Finish the penguin.

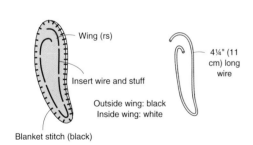

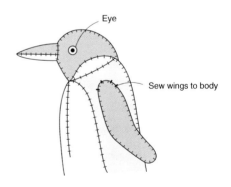

1. Bend wire into shape of wing. Align one black and one white **wing** piece and sew, inserting wire and stuffing as you work. Repeat for other **wing**.

2. Sew wings to **body sides**. Refer to page 40 to make and attach eyes.

Polar Bears: Cub

Shown on page 28

Cutting Instructions

Trace and cut out the following templates on pattern sheet B:

Off-White Felt
- Head (cut 1)
- Muzzle (cut 1)
- Body bottom (cut 1)
- Body side (cut 2)
- Soles (cut 4)
- Body top (cut 1)

- Ears (cut 2)
- Tail top (cut 1)
- Tail bottom (cut 1)

Light Gray Felt
- Ears (cut 2)

Materials

- Felt pieces
  - Off-white: 8" x 8" (20 x 20 cm)
  - Light gray: ⅜" x ¾" (1 x 2 cm)
- Machine sewing thread in black and off-white
- 6-strand embroidery floss in black
- 8" (20 cm) of 21-gauge plastic wire
- Two ¼" (0.4 cm) diameter black eye buttons
- Polyester stuffing
- Quick-dry tacky glue

Finished Project

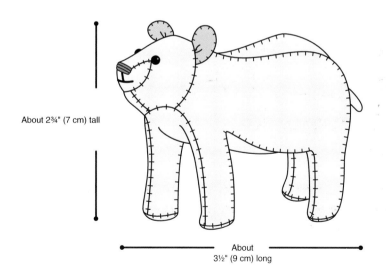

About 2¾" (7 cm) tall

About 3½" (9 cm) long

Make the head and body.

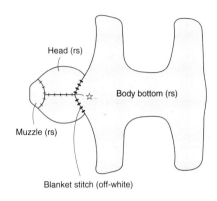

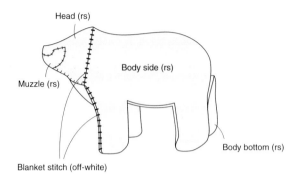

1. Refer to page 119 to make **head**. Align **head** with **body bottom** (☆) and sew.

2. Align one **body side** with **head** and **body bottom** and sew along neck and front leg. Repeat for other **body side**.

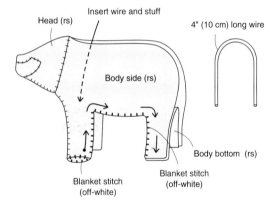

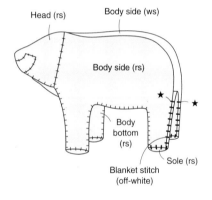

3. Align one **body side** with **body bottom** and sew from front leg to back leg. Repeat for other **body side**. Align **soles** with front legs and sew. Bend two wires into U-shaped pieces. Stuff front paws. Insert wire into front legs and stuff.

4. Align each **body side** with **body bottom** and sew along back legs. Align **soles** with back legs and sew. Stuff back paws. Insert other wire and stuff.

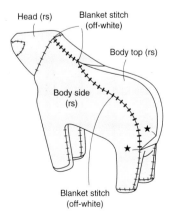

5. Align one **body side** with **body top** and sew. Sew two **body sides** together along neck.

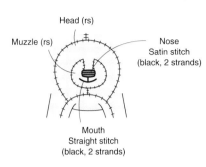

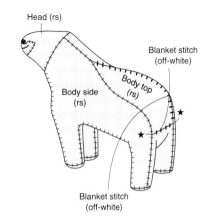

6. Stuff head. Embroider nose and mouth. Hide knots in stuffing.

7. Align remaining **body side** with **body top** and sew, stuffing as you work. Stuff bottom and sew polar bear closed along rear end.

Finish the face.

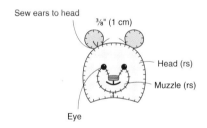

1. Refer to page 121 to make **ears**. Use a large needle to puncture holes in head at positions to attach eyes. Insert eye buttons and glue to secure.

Make the tail.

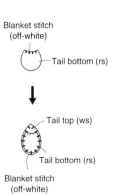

1. Sew along top edge of **tail bottom**. Align **tail top** with **tail bottom** and sew, stuffing lightly as you work.

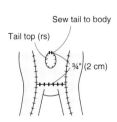

2. Sew tail to body, about ¾" (2 cm) from bottom seam.

Materials

- Felt pieces
    - Off-white: Three 8" x 8" (20 x 20 cm)
    - Light gray: ¾" x 1 ½" (2 x 4 cm)
    - Black: ⅜" x ¾" (1 x 2 cm)
    - Beige: ⅜" x ¾" (1 x 2 cm)
- Machine sewing thread in black and off-white
- 6-strand embroidery floss in dark gray
- 15¾" (40 cm) of 21-gauge plastic wire
- Two ¼" (0.4 cm) diameter black eye buttons
- Polyester stuffing
- Quick-dry tacky glue

Polar Bears: Adult

Shown on page 28

Cutting Instructions

Trace and cut out the following templates on pattern sheet B:

Off-White Felt
- Head (cut 1)
- Muzzle (cut 1)
- Neck (cut 2)
- Body side (cut 2)
- Body bottom (cut 1)
- Soles (cut 4)
- Body top (cut 1)
- Ears (cut 2)
- Tail top (cut 1)
- Tail bottom (cut 1)

Light Gray Felt
- Ears (cut 2)

Black Felt
- Nose (cut 2)

Beige Felt
- Eye pieces (cut 2)

Finished Project

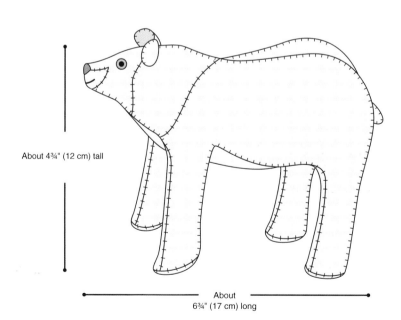

About 4¾" (12 cm) tall

About 6¾" (17 cm) long

Make the head.

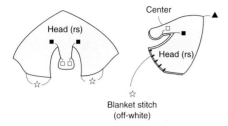 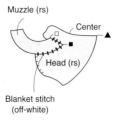

1. Sew **head** edges together at chin.

2. Align **head** with **muzzle** (■) and sew together on three sides.

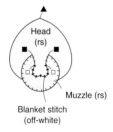 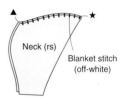

3. Sew **head** and **muzzle** together around nose.

4. Sew two **neck** pieces together along upper edge.

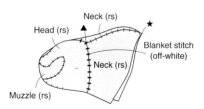 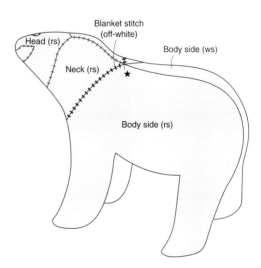

5. Align **head** with **neck** (▲) and sew.

6. Align **neck** with each **body side** (★) and sew.

Make the body.

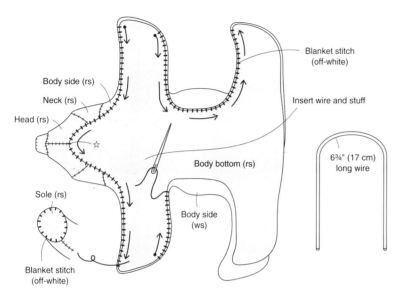

Blanket stitch (off-white)

Body side (rs)

Neck (rs)

Head (rs)

Insert wire and stuff

Body bottom (rs)

Sole (rs)

Body side (ws)

Blanket stitch (off-white)

6¾" (17 cm) long wire

1. Align **body bottom** with polar bear and sew together, stopping at inner back legs. Align **soles** with front legs and sew. Bend two wires into U-shapes. Insert one wire into front legs. Stuff front legs, head, and neck.

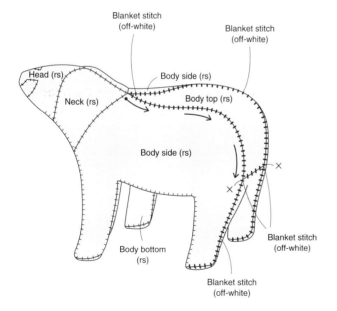

Blanket stitch (off-white)

Blanket stitch (off-white)

Head (rs)

Body side (rs)

Neck (rs)

Body top (rs)

Body side (rs)

Body bottom (rs)

Blanket stitch (off-white)

Blanket stitch (off-white)

2. Align one **body side** with **body top** and sew. Repeat for other **body side**, stuffing as you work. Align each **body side** with **body bottom** and sew together along back legs. Align **soles** with back legs and sew. Insert other plastic wire and stuff. Stuff bottom and sew polar bear closed along rear end.

Finish the face.

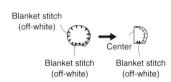

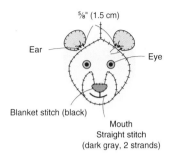

1. For each **ear**, layer two colors of felt and sew together around all edges. Fold each ear in half inwardly and sew across base using two stitches to secure fold.

2. Sew ears to head, about ⅝" (1.5 cm) apart. Refer to page 40 to make and attach eyes. Sew two **nose** pieces together, stuffing lightly as you work. Sew nose to head. Embroider mouth. Hide knot in stuffing.

Make the tail.

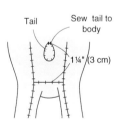

1. Refer to page 117 to make **tail**. Sew tail to body, about 1¼" (3 cm) from bottom seam.

Dolphin $\quad$ Shown on page 30

Cutting Instructions

Trace and cut out the following templates on pattern sheet B:

Gray Felt
- Body side (cut 2)
- Outside nose top (cut 1)
- Nose top base (cut 1)
- Tail top (cut 2)
- Tail bottom (cut 1)

Off-White Felt
- Outside nose bottom (cut 1)
- Nose bottom base (cut 1)
- Body bottom (cut 1)

Pink Felt
- Inside nose top (cut 1)
- Inside nose bottom (cut 1)

Light Brown Felt
- Eye pieces (cut 2)

Materials

- Felt pieces
  - Gray: 8" x 8" (20 x 20 cm)
  - Off-white: 1¼" x 4¼" (3 x 11 cm)
  - Pink: 2" x 2¾" (5 x 7 cm)
  - Light brown: ⅜" x ¾" (1 x 2 cm)
- Machine sewing thread in gray and off-white
- 11¾" (30 cm) of 21-gauge plastic wire
- Two ¼" (0.4 cm) diameter black eye buttons
- Polyester stuffing
- Quick-dry tacky glue

Finished Project

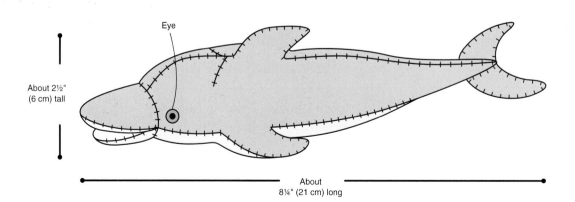

Eye

About 2½" (6 cm) tall

About 8¼" (21 cm) long

Sew the sides together.

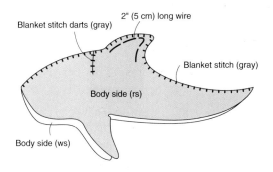

1. On each **body side**, align darts and sew. Sew two **body sides** together along top. Bend wire into shape of fin. Insert wire and stuff fin.

Make the nose.

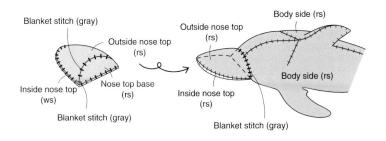

1. Align **outside nose top** with **nose top base** and sew. Align **inside nose top** with this piece and sew, stuffing as you work. Sew nose top to dolphin.

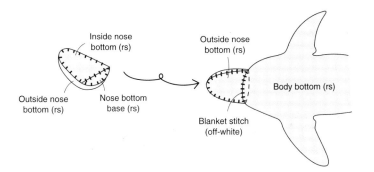

2. Make nose bottom following same process used for nose top. Align nose bottom with **body bottom** and sew.

Make the tail.

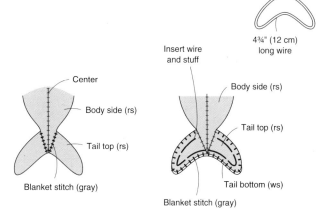

1. Align each **body side** with a **tail top** piece and sew. Align **tail bottom** with **tail top** and sew.

Finish the nose.

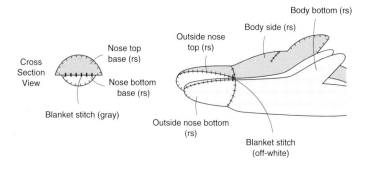

1. Working from inside of dolphin, align **nose bases** and sew. On outside of dolphin, align **nose top** with **nose bottom** so top covers bottom and stitch to secure. Repeat for other side.

Finish the dolphin.

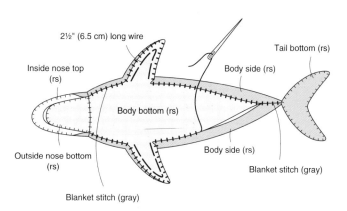

1. Bend two wires into shape of flippers. Align one **body side** with **body bottom** and sew, inserting plastic wires and stuffing as you work. Repeat for other **body side**. Sew two **body sides** together along tail. Refer to page 40 to make and attach eyes, as shown in finished project diagram on page 122.

Materials

- Felt pieces
  - Hot pink: 6" x 6" (15 x 15 cm)
  - Light yellow: 4" x 4" (10 x 10 cm)
  - Light green: ⅜" x ¾" (1 x 2 cm)
- Machine sewing thread in pink and light beige
- 6-strand embroidery floss in black
- 11¾" (30 cm) of 21-gauge plastic wire
- Cardboard: 1¼" x 2 ½" (3 x 6 cm)
- Two ⅛" (0.3 cm) diameter black eye buttons
- Polyester stuffing
- Quick-dry tacky glue
- Scotch tape

Flamingo

Shown on page 32

Cutting Instructions

Trace and cut out the following templates on pattern sheet B:

Hot Pink Felt
- Body side (cut 2)
- Body bottom (cut 1)
- Body top (cut 1)
- Wings (cut 4)

Light Yellow Felt
- Beak (cut 2)
- Legs (cut 4)

- Foot top (cut 2)
- Foot bottom (cut 2)

Light Green Felt
- Eye pieces (cut 2)

Cardboard
- Foot (cut 2)

Finished Project

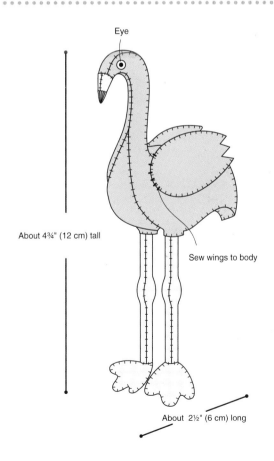

Eye

About 4¾" (12 cm) tall

Sew wings to body

About 2½" (6 cm) long

Make the body.

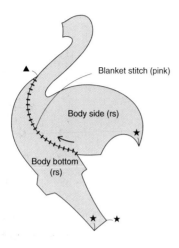

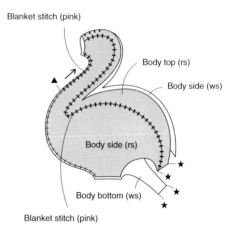

1. Align one **body side** with **body bottom** and sew. Repeat for other **body side**.

2. Align two **body sides** along neck (▲) and sew together. Align one **body side** with one **body top** and sew. On other side, sew pieces together for 4-5 stitches only. Do not cut thread.

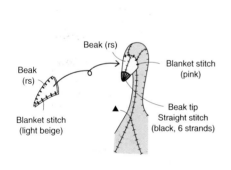

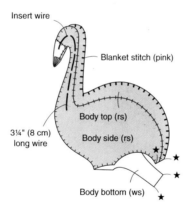

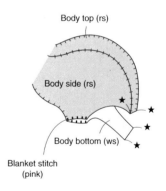

3. Sew two **beak** pieces together, stuff, and sew to head. Embroider beak tip. Hide knot in stuffing.

4. Bend a wire into shape of head and neck. Align remaining **body side** with **body top** and sew to rear end. Insert wire and stuff.

5. Sew around each leg opening.

Make the legs and attach the wings.

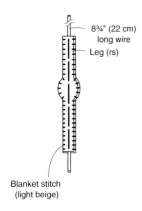

8¾" (22 cm) long wire
Leg (rs)
Blanket stitch (light beige)

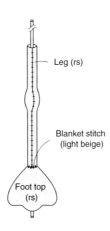

Leg (rs)
Blanket stitch (light beige)
Foot top (rs)

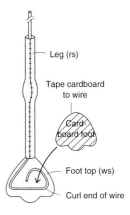

Leg (rs)
Tape cardboard to wire
Cardboard foot
Foot top (ws)
Curl end of wire

1. Insert a wire between two **leg** pieces. Sew, stuffing as you work.

2. Align **leg** with one **foot top** and sew.

3. Curl end of wire into shape of foot. Tape a **cardboard foot** to wire.

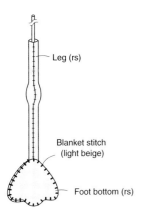

Leg (rs)
Blanket stitch (light beige)
Foot bottom (rs)

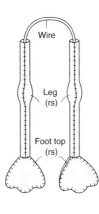

Wire
Leg (rs)
Foot top (rs)

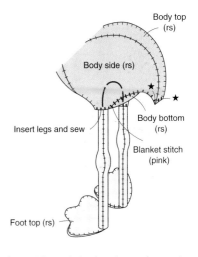

Body top (rs)
Body side (rs)
★
★
Body bottom (rs)
Blanket stitch (pink)
Insert legs and sew
Foot top (rs)

4. Align **foot bottom** with **foot top** and sew.

5. Make other **leg** following same process. Note: both legs share the 8¾" (22 cm) long wire.

6. Insert **legs** into body and sew to secure. Stuff bottom. Align **body top, bottom, and sides** (★) and sew flamingo closed.

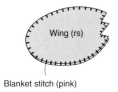

Wing (rs)
Blanket stitch (pink)

7. For each **wing**, sew two wing pieces together and sew to **body sides**, as shown in finished project diagram on page 125. Refer to page 40 to make and attach eyes.

A DAVID & CHARLES BOOK

© 2010 Tomomi Maeda

All rights reserved. The written instructions, photographs, designs, and projects in this volume
are intended for the personal use of the reader and may be reproduced for that purpose only.
Any other use, especially commercial use, is forbidden under law without the express written
permission of the copyright holder. Violators will be prosecuted to the fullest extent of the law.
No other part of this book may be reproduced in any form or by any electronic or mechanical
means including information storage and retrieval systems without permission in writing from the
publisher, except by a reviewer, who may quote a brief passage in review.

The information in this book was originally published in the following title:
20 CM NO FELT DE TSUKURU DOUBUTSU (NV80089)
© 2010 Tomomi Maeda © NIHON VOGUE-SHA 2010
Photography: Akiko Ohshima
Originally published in Japanese language by Nihon Vogue Co., LTD.

All rights reserved. No part of this book may be reproduced in any form without written
permission from the original proprietor.

English language translation & production by World Book Media, LLC.
Email: info@worldbookmedia.com
Translated by Kyoko Matthews

First published in the UK and USA in 2013 by F&W Media International, LTD.

David & Charles is an imprint of F&W Media International, LTD.
Brunel House, Forde Close, Newton Abbot, TQ12 4PU, UK

F&W Media International, Ltd is a subsidiary of F+W Media, Inc
10151 Carver Road, Suite #200, Blue Ash, OH 45242, USA

ISBN-13: 978-1-4463-0265-1 paperback
ISBN-10: 1-4463-0265-2 paperback
Printed in China

F+W Media publishes high quality books on a wide range of subjects.
For more great book ideas visit: www.stitchcraftcreate.co.uk

CALGARY PUBLIC LIBRARY

3 9065 13846047 0